How to Fight Inequality

To all those who won the fight against inequality before, and who will win it again: extraordinary, ordinary, people.

'Ben Phillips has helped bring global attention to the inequality crisis. *How to Fight Inequality* is an ideal guide for anyone who wants to help. He brings to the book lessons and stories from a lifetime deeply enmeshed in activism and organizing, finding hope not in famous leaders but in everyday people, and setting out how each of us can get engaged in building a more equal society.'

Naila Kabeer

'Ben Phillips is a stalwart campaigner for a fairer world. *How to Fight Inequality* is a handy primer to help people to build power together.'

John Githongo

'We now know just how harmful inequality is to us all. But can anything be done about it? Ben Phillips' smart new book is packed with powerful stories of change won from the ground up, helps guide us in what we can do by organizing together, and demonstrates that a more equal future is ours to make.'

Kate Pickett

'Inequality defines our present but it is not our fate. In Ben Phillips' crisp guide, he shows from past victories and today's vibrant new movements a way we can win. His first-hand stories of "extraordinary, ordinary people" winning change illustrate how, together, we have the power to beat inequality.'

Kumi Naidoo

'Most of us know how severe – and how dangerous – inequality has become. The debates have been won, but the problem keeps getting worse. Now we must win the fight. And there can be no spectators: it is up to you and me to make change happen. As US President Lyndon Johnson once told Martin Luther King: "I know what I have to do – but you have to make me do it." Ben Phillips' short, sharp, powerful book provides a rousing call for action, and draws on the hard lessons of history to create an essential how-to guide to what works and what doesn't, in the epoch-defying struggle of our new gilded age.'

Nicholas Shaxson

About the Author

Ben Phillips has combined the roles of NGO director, political advisor, civil society activist, and writer. He has lived and worked in four continents and fourteen cities.

He began his development work at the grassroots, as a teacher and ANC activist living in Mamelodi township, South Africa, in 1994, just after the end of apartheid.

He has led programmes and campaigns teams in Oxfam, ActionAid, Save the Children, the Children's Society, the Global Call to Action Against Poverty and the Global Campaign for Education. He has addressed the United Nations and been appointed to the Civil Society Advisory Committee of the United Nations Development Programme.

He co-founded the Fight Inequality Alliance, the growing movement for a more equal world, that brings major NGOs together with social movements, rights activists, environmentalists, women's groups, faith groups and trade unions, to campaign together for action on economic and social inequality.

He advises the UN and governments from across the world on how inequality can be beaten.

He has been the Hewlett Fellow of Public Policy at the Kellogg Institute at Notre Dame, the Resident Fellow on inequality at the Rockefeller Foundation's Bellagio Center, and the guest lecturer on global inequality for the Cambridge University series and book *Capitalism on the Edge*.

He has written for the *Guardian*, the *Financial Times*, the *New Internationalist* and Reuters, among others, and appeared regularly on TV, including on CNN, Al Jazeera and the BBC.

He tweets at @benphillips76.

How to Fight Inequality

(and Why That Fight Needs You)

Ben Phillips

polity

First published in 2020 by Polity Press

Reprinted 2020, 2021

Polity Press
65 Bridge Street
Cambridge CB2 1UR, UK

Polity Press
101 Station Landing
Suite 300
Medford, MA 02155, USA

ISBN-13: 978-1-5095-4308-3
ISBN-13: 978-1-5095-4309-0 (pb)

A catalogue record for this book is available from the British Library.

Library of Congress Cataloging-in-Publication Data
Names: Phillips, Ben (Civil society activist), author.
Title: How to fight inequality : (and why that fight needs you) / Ben Phillips.
Description: Medford : Polity, 2020. | Includes bibliographical references and index. | Summary: "A DIY-guide to tackling inequality for activists everywhere"-- Provided by publisher.
Identifiers: LCCN 2020010435 (print) | LCCN 2020010436 (ebook) | ISBN 9781509543083 (hardback) | ISBN 9781509543090 (paperback) | ISBN 9781509543106 (epub)
Subjects: LCSH: Equality. | Income distribution. | Elite (Social sciences)--History--21st century. | Social policy.
Classification: LCC HM821 .P485 2020 (print) | LCC HM821 (ebook) | DDC 361.2/5--dc23
LC record available at https://lccn.loc.gov/2020010435
LC ebook record available at https://lccn.loc.gov/2020010436

Typeset in 11 on 14pt Sabon
by Fakenham Prepress Solutions, Fakenham, Norfolk NR21 8NL
Printed and bound in the United States by LSC Communications

For further information on Polity, visit our website:
politybooks.com

Contents

Acknowledgements

Though this book is a personal reflection and all mistakes are my own, I do not feel that I own this book alone. Writing it has depended most of all on amazing grassroots organizers sharing their stories, hosting me in their communities, and teaching me what they have learnt from the messiness of getting involved. Some are featured in the stories in this book – I hope that those stories help to share their wisdom. A huge thank you, also, to those organizers and activists whose stories are not in this book but who have inspired it through their lived example.

I started sharing some of these stories in talks and then in articles because people told me that hearing about other people's struggles, setbacks and successes in the fight against inequality helped them to make a difference. I had not originally envisaged creating a book.

Then, when I arrived at a retreat with other writers, I was starstruck to find that one of my fellow residents was my favourite novelist, Kiran Desai. So when she insisted that there was a book there that needed to

Acknowledgements

be written, helped me envisage what it could be, and insisted that I would be able to produce it if I persisted, I couldn't not write it.

The Bellagio Center and then the Kellogg Institute generously provided the physical space (and skilfully enabled the head space) to write. George Owers and Julia Davies at Polity Press modelled the tough love vital in editors.

I am hugely grateful for the insights of so many wonderful people who are part of Oxfam, ActionAid, the Fight Inequality Alliance, the United Nations, and the Center on International Cooperation.

I am forever indebted to the Usawa crew in Nairobi, the Notre Dame and South Bend folks, and the El Salvador Romereanos.

Additionally, many expert writers were generous in response to my requests for advice, and it is impossible to list everyone, but amongst those who gave especially of their time are: Sr. Helen Alford, Matthew Bolton, Winnie Byanyima, Hector Castañón, Sarah Cliffe, Alex Cobham, Nicholas Colloff, Pedro Conceição, Abby Córdova, Ashvin Dayal, Mike Edwards, Alice Evans, Marshall Ganz, John Githongo, Jonathan Glennie, Duncan Green, CJ Grimes, Michael Higgins, Alison Hirsh, Irungu Houghton, Naila Kabeer, Tamara Kay, Thea Lee, Kelsea Marie-Pim, Richard Murphy, Savior Mwamba, Jay Naidoo, Kumi Naidoo, Ray Offenheiser, Isabel Ortiz, Ann Pettifor, Kate Pickett, Rakesh Rajani, Kavita Ramdas, Diego Sánchez-Ancochea, Mike Savage, Nicholas Shaxson, Rebecca Simson, Bev Skeggs, Andy Sumner, Robin Varghese, Tuca Vieira and Rana Zincair-Celal.

Geeta Bandi-Phillips has been an insightful commentator and wise counsel, both for the book and for its author. As our kids, Ashoka and Sanghamitra, have grown, it has been inspiring to explore the ideas in the book with them too: in their own activism, in the daily kindness that they show to those around them, and in their rightful challenging of us, they and their generation fill me with great hope. We owe it to their generation to repay that hope – not only by cheering them on, but by walking alongside them.

'I don't think this world was made for a small minority to dance on the faces of everyone else.'

H.G. Wells

'I am no longer accepting the things I cannot change, I am changing the things I cannot accept.'

Angela Davis

'The quality of justice depends on the equality of power to compel.'

Thucydides

Introduction

Inequality is the fight of our time
Winning the fight needs you
This book is to help you win the fight

Inequality is the fight of our time

Let's start off with a quiz. What period was the author of the words below describing, and who was the author?

> While the earnings of a minority are growing exponentially, so too is the gap separating the majority from the prosperity enjoyed by those happy few. The powerful feed upon the powerless. Masses of people find themselves excluded and marginalized: without work, without possibilities, without any means of escape. Finance, special interests and economic interests are trumping the common good so their own plans will not be affected. Inequality is the root of social evil.

Some guess the nineteenth century, and think it must be Marx, or perhaps Dickens. But the period being

1

described is now, and the author is the Pope. And he's bang on the money.

In the Covid-19 crisis, we have seen an exacerbation of the challenges we face. We have witnessed, in ever starker view, the inverse relationship between the concentration of wealth and social contribution. We have watched key workers without proper protections hold our society together, while elites look after themselves and make scapegoats of society's most vulnerable people. We have seen the immorality and unsustainability of systems in which our right to life is shaped by our bank balance. The acute crisis of the present moment, Covid-19, has revealed the deeper crisis of our age: inequality.

Widening inequality – and how we start to beat it – is the defining struggle of our time. We are living in an inequality crisis, and it could break us. Economically, we are seeing in many countries trajectories of extreme concentrations of wealth and power in the hands of a few that hark back to a century ago. Politically, we are seeing governments loosening their watch over major corporations and big finance, and tightening their watch over unions, community organizations, non-governmental organizations (NGOs) and citizens. The new golden rule is that those with the gold make the rules. Socially, too, we are seeing how an increasingly divided world is becoming an increasingly angry, intolerant and violent one. Ecologically, inequality is driving us to the climate's tipping point and undermining moves to prevent catastrophe. The world is in danger not just of a slow-down in social progress but of a reversal of it.

Building up from seeing the consequences of widening inequality over the past few decades, then spurred dramatically in the years following the 2008 crash, a growing chorus of people pushed to get the inequality crisis recognized as real, damaging and needing to be tackled. And yet even at that time, in calling out inequality, they faced great push back and were labelled as extremists. Organizations received clear messages from governments, donors and even their own boards to stop being outspoken about inequality.

And then, in what seemed like a very short time in a few years either side of 2015, governments and establishment institutions across the world suddenly shifted en masse and said that they agreed. Now, for example, today's inequalities are recognized as harmful and dangerous by mainstream economists, the IMF, the World Bank, the Organisation for Economic Co-operation and Development (OECD) and even the World Economic Forum; and all governments have, in signing the UN Sustainable Development Goals in 2015, pledged to reduce inequality. We have, rightly, celebrated these victories.

But winning on words has not meant winning on action. Inequalities continue to worsen, and the broad thrust of government action is at best insufficient to address them. Securing official consensus has not, on its own, led to inequalities being tackled. We face now the contradiction that every world leader has promised to act on inequality and yet only a handful of them are doing anything about it. Where to go from here?

In discussions with those academics and policy wonks who propose 'generating more evidence' as the answer to tackling inequality, I like to tease them by highlighting what I call the 'evidence-based paradox': (1) We should be evidenced-based in our approaches.

(2) The evidence for transformational change happening *because decision-makers are shown evidence* is really weak. Therefore, (3) if we are truly-evidenced based, we will not depend only on evidence-sharing as a strategy for change. The problem we face in beating inequality is *not* that we do not know what needs to be done, it's that we haven't brought together the collective power to overcome those who are stopping it from being done.

Evidence is not enough. Policy proposals are not enough. Being right is not enough. Formal agreement is not enough. The change needed to address inequality won't be achieved by piling up so many reports that power gracefully gives in to intellectual prowess, nor by befriending a few officials with smooth insider advocacy. The genteel world of debate is not enough to shift the much harsher world of interests. As Upton Sinclair wrote, 'it is difficult to get a man to understand something, when his salary depends on his not understanding it.' To secure real change we have to get engaged in what's called the 'political economy' of inequality – that is, not just participate in the surface formal discussion, but understand how power is maintained and work out how we can challenge it. Inequality is the fight of our time.

Winning the fight needs you

While it is clear that some leaders made commitments to tackle inequality without an intention to implement them, it is also the case that even the most well-intentioned leaders need popular pressure. My analysis, that we can't rely on political leaders to bring change for us, has been taken by some to imply a view that all policy-makers are venal and uncaring; but that's not my experience, nor is it my argument; rather, the point is that having good policy-makers is not enough to shift inequality – there are too many pressures on them from the interests at the top, which need a countervailing pressure from below. Remember the story of President Lyndon Johnson telling Martin Luther King 'I know what I have to do, but you have to make me do it.'

As I shared with the Inter-Parliamentary Union of elected politicians from across the world when they invited me to address them, as an ally, pressure on leaders from below is going to be awkward sometimes. I know that there is a sense among some in government that sometimes activists can be seen as too 'rambunctious' and 'loud', and that they 'don't behave', but when we ask, for example, why did South Africa get to have the largest anti-retroviral programme in the world, keeping millions of people alive, when we ask how did India get to have one of the best right to information laws in the world, we know that the reason is because of 'awkward', 'difficult', social movements causing a fuss. This is a historical fact.

Likewise, the reason we need to challenge the power of economic elites is *not* because they are personally uncompassionate, but because elite compassion has never been enough to beat inequality. Inequality is so hard to break because it is a vicious cycle: the power imbalance that comes with the concentration of wealth – and its interaction with politics, economics, society and narrative – enables the further concentration of wealth and a worsened power imbalance. History shows that inequality can be beaten, but it also shows us that this depends on securing a shift in who shapes the big decisions – and that that will only be possible when enough of us get together to overcome deference, build our collective power, and create a new story.

We can sometimes feel that things are all going on *around* us, but we can *shape* them too – not alone, but with each other. If there is one generalizable lesson of social change it seems to be this: no one saves others, people standing together is how they liberate themselves. It can be slow and it's always complicated and it sometimes fails – but it's the only way it works. Kumi Naidoo, the South African organizer who has led Greenpeace and Amnesty, put it to me this way: 'we've spent too many years looking upwards at governments, we have to change our gaze and focus on people's organizing.' The structure will not change from the top. As young activists expressed it to me: 'There is no justice, just us.' But 'just us' – organized – is powerful.

Importantly, people power is *not* about depending on great popular leaders. In shifting from hoping elites will unseat *themselves*, to seeing that change will come from *movements*, we mustn't *then* make the mistake of hoping that social transformation will be delivered by charismatic individuals greater than ourselves. Organizers from countries across the world have all told me variations of this vital lesson: 'people are often looking for a redeemer, but it is we who will redeem ourselves.' To succeed, people's movements really have to be *people's* movements. The real primary role of those highlighted as great popular leaders is as expressions of the work of many others. As Archbishop Desmond Tutu, with all love and honour, famously said of Nelson Mandela: 'He is only one pebble on the beach, one of thousands; not an insignificant pebble, I'll grant you that, but a pebble all the same.' Indeed, Mandela himself regularly recalled that when most of the leading ANC figures were in prison or in exile, it was ordinary workers, priests and even schoolchildren who had carried on the struggle.

As a young volunteer in a South African township just after the end of apartheid, I was privileged to learn from the people with whom I lived how they had beaten apartheid, by holding strong together, through protests, strikes and organizing, building their collective power through solidarity across groups – churches, unions, citizens' organizations – and making connections internationally. They took me to hear Mandela speak at rallies, and hearing him there I realized two things. Firstly, I knew that I *was* in the presence of a hero. But more importantly, as I looked around those rallies, I realized that I was in the presence of *thousands* of heroes – and learnt that change doesn't come from one great leader but from people building power together.

In the most transformational movements that I have had the privilege to be part of, people gather in a circle, see that they are not alone, and start to talk. And from that the most powerful actions build. The change we need won't be given to people, it will be fought for by people. This is a lesson learnt by others who struggled against inequality in the past. As Frederick Douglass, former slave and great anti-slavery campaigner, told his audience in 1857:

> The whole history of the progress shows that all concessions have been born of earnest struggle. The conflict has been exciting, agitating, all-absorbing, and for the time being, putting all other tumults to silence. It must

do this, or it does nothing. If there is no struggle there is no progress. Those who profess to favor freedom and yet deprecate agitation want crops without plowing up the ground; rain without thunder and lightning. They want the ocean without the awful roar of its many waters. Power concedes nothing without a demand. It never did and it never will.

Winning the fight against inequality needs you.

This book is to help you win the fight

There have been many excellent books on how inequality has gotten so extreme, why it is harmful, and what kind of policies could help tackle inequality, and to all of those books the cause of tackling inequality is deeply indebted; but *this* book seeks to build on the recent recognition of *inequality as a problem* (which it is, and which is now established), to addressing the paradox that *the mainstream consensus has shifted to recognize the inequality crisis without a consequent sufficient shift in action.* It seeks to complement the 'what'-focused arguments which dominate the literature on inequality, with 'how'-focused arguments about the ways to advance the *social processes* to build the *context* that will see inequality turned around – after all, the 'policy' agenda to tackle inequality will only be realized if the fight is won. Most books on inequality are about what *other people* ought to do about it – this book is about what you can do about it, and is written to help you do it as effectively as possible.

I don't pretend to be a cold detached third-party expert observer doing highly technical social science.

Indeed, the tendency of work on tackling inequality to drift into the arcane policy-academic space holds back the catalysing of organizing on the scale needed. Instead, I write as an organizer sharing what I have learnt from others and witnessed.

My varied roles have included working at the grassroots, leading campaigns, serving on the senior leadership of major international NGOs like Oxfam and ActionAid, co-founding coalitions and movements including the Fight Inequality Alliance, and advising governments and the UN. Through these I have been able to get a close-up view, in countries across the world, of the huge challenge of inequality and of the inspiring organizers taking it on. I have learnt most from having been able to directly witness people uniting to fight inequality and some moments of progress, pain and amusement. This book takes you with me to meet the extraordinary ordinary people, past and present, who have shown how transformational change can be won.

Given the overwhelming evidence on inequality, the new high-level consensus, and the pledge by every government in the world to tackle it under the internationally agreed UN Sustainable Development Goals, the book isn't designed to persuade those who still champion keeping inequality on its current trajectory; I don't think that a book *could* do that. This book is aimed at helping those who *want* a more equal world to *achieve* it. It is not written mainly to persuade *people in power*, but instead to help build the *power of the people*.

The book is ultimately optimistic. I *do* set out plainly how inequality is heading in a very dangerous direction for everyone, and how it will not self-correct. Though that can be hard for people to hear, it is vital to communicate the evidence of harm. But while some have argued that rising inequality is unavoidable, or that it has gone so far now it can't be reversed or can only be reversed after catastrophe, this book shows that these are false. I share the stories of people's 'agency' that show how we can change the direction of inequality, together.

The book is not only a moral call to action, but draws on global experience to answer three big questions in turn: *why* we need to win the fight against inequality; how we won the fight against inequality *before*; and how we'll win the fight against inequality *again*. In this way, the book is both an *argument* – that only people power can tackle inequality – and a *guide* – how we can do it.

My aim is not merely to inform people or even to persuade them to agree with a point of view. My aim is to help people to *take action*, as effectively as possible. There are no spectators! For the many of you reading this book who are already involved in the fight against inequality, this book is to help you make even more of a difference. For others reading this who may not yet be involved in the fight against it, this book is to help you to join in well.

Why we need to win the fight against inequality

How inequality is worsening
How inequality harms us all
How we won the debate
Why winning the debate is not enough and we have
to win the fight

How inequality is worsening

Let's do another quiz. Where is this?

Why we need to win the fight against inequality

This photograph, showing a slum abutting a luxury high-rise apartment block, complete with balcony swimming pools on every storey, is one I have shown to groups around the world. I ask people where it is, and overwhelmingly people guess wrong. They often name their own city. That's not a fault on their part, it's an illustration of how common this stark division is. This particular picture happens to be São Paulo – it is the 'border' between the favela of Paraisópolis and the affluent district of Morumbi, taken by the great Brazilian photojournalist Tuca Vieira. But it could just as easily be Nairobi, or Delhi, or Bangkok, or Islamabad, or Lagos, or Jo'burg; they all look as divided as this.

When I mentioned to Tuca that people from so many different countries kept thinking that his photo was of their city, he was clear why: 'it's an image that is universal, because it shows how inequality is the actual form of globalization that we have received. We were told to expect something very liberating, but instead we have been delivered a demarcation between an increasingly homogenized rich on one side and the rest of us on the other side.' It's not just a money separation, it's also a physical separation, and a social and cultural separation – a brutal divide.

Extreme economic inequality has exploded across the world in the last three to four decades. Seven out of ten people live in countries where the gap between rich and poor is greater than it was 30 years ago. As I saw for myself in Zambia when I met with dispossessed farmers there, while the country has been moving from officially poor to officially middle income, the number of poor people has actually increased. In

Pakistan, half the population has no land, while just 5 per cent of landowners have two thirds of the land; in the cities the top 20 per cent of the population accounts for over 60 per cent of earned income, while the bottom 20 per cent makes do on just 3 per cent. In the US, the richest 10 per cent of the population captured all of the growth that followed the recession. In fact, the rich captured *more* than all the growth, and the other 90 per cent went *backwards*. Credit Suisse has estimated the share of wealth that is held by the richest 1 per cent as being almost 50 per cent in Indonesia, 60 per cent in India and Thailand, and 75 per cent in Russia.

When Occupy first started to popularize the term 'the one per cent' they were accused of exaggerating just how much was held by a very few. In fact, they were understating how concentrated wealth is – as within the one per cent a much smaller number dominate. An important aspect of inequality highlighted in recent studies, going beyond the traditional Gini measures which don't shed much light on the very top, is the breaking away in recent decades of these fractions, the people who are said to inherit 'the stratosphere'. Branko Milavonić highlights this difference between a millionaire and a billionaire with this illustration: 'Suppose that you inherited either $1 million or $1 billion, and that you spent $1,000 every day. It would take you less than three years to run through your inheritance in the first case, and nearly 2,700 years ... in the second case.' It is unimaginable, unspendable and un*earnable* wealth.

People were shocked when it was revealed that the 300 richest people have the same wealth as the poorest half of the world. But then that number holding wealth equivalent to half the world was revealed to have concentrated even further: the crack research team I was privileged to oversee at Oxfam famously showed it was just 85, and by 2019 the number of people holding the same wealth as the poorest half of the world had gone down to only 26, overwhelmingly white men. These stark global figures can be seen at regional and national levels too. In Africa the 10 richest families have the same wealth as the poorest half of that continent.

In Manhattan I went to meet Morris Pearl, a multi-millionaire former BlackRock executive. Morris's frankness was bracing. He ripped apart the standard story about how such fortunes reflect the fair reward of hard work: 'The wealth of people like me has become self-perpetuating. I quit my business work five years ago and yet I am wealthier now than I was then. My son, who has been studying, has also gotten wealthier. Now even our money is making money. On top of that, we pay lower taxes than people with a lot less. And governments organize laws around ensuring that this spiral of inequality continues ever upwards. Does having government serve the rich in this way benefit the wider economy? Absolutely not.' His final line was the kicker: 'This situation is dangerous – for everyone. If unaddressed, this kind of thing doesn't end well.'

How inequality harms us all

The consequences of this gap between the richest and the rest have been manifold. Indeed, there are so many reasons why rising inequality is a bad thing that it's hard to know where to start.

One reason, as King's College London economist Andy Sumner has demonstrated, is that 'we find in our number-crunching that poverty can only be ended if inequality falls.' Tackling inequality is key to tackling poverty – both because extreme and growing economic inequality undermines poverty reduction and because the warping of power towards the one per cent is shifting the focus of governments towards corporations and away from their citizens.

Defenders of rising inequality claim that it is growth which ends poverty, and that it is rising inequality, among other things, which enables growth. But both these claims have been shown to be false. Rising inequality has weakened progress on poverty reduction. On its own, growth is not good enough – indeed in many cases growth has seemingly been decoupled from enabling decent jobs and the broad benefit for ordinary people. Papua New Guinea recently experienced the highest growth in the world and yet didn't meet any of the UN's globally-agreed Millennium Development Goals on tackling poverty, because the proceeds of growth were so unequally shared. South Africa's ANC won plaudits for economic responsibility when it abandoned the redistributive calls of the Freedom Charter – and now the gap between rich and poor is worse than it was at the end of apartheid. Angola has experienced a staggering annual growth rate of around

25 per cent and yet retained one of the highest infant mortality rates in the world. Britain's former Secretary of State for International Development has not been alone in saying of the relationship between growth and poverty reduction: 'It really is that simple.' But it isn't.

The inequality crisis is not only hurting people in the Global South. The protections and the moderation of inequality brought in across the Global North with the post-war consensus have also been ruptured. In Mediterranean Europe, the EU and the IMF imposed brutal reductions on living standards that saw massive pauperization and social dislocation and brought back to the people of the region medical conditions like rickets once thought consigned to the history books. The IMF responded to critics by saying that they couldn't sympathize with Greeks as real poverty was in Africa. But African civil society organizations responded with more empathy and more insight by pointing out that poverty in Mediterranean Europe was getting so bad because the structural adjustment approach once foisted on Africans was now getting foisted on Southern Europeans.

Even before the financial crisis began, inequality was on the rise. And the only people who weren't hit by the financial crisis, the data shows, were *the financiers*. The men who caused the financial crisis ended up better off now than they were the day before the crash. Just five years after the collapse of Bear Stearns, the firm's former bosses were back in major roles on Wall Street.

In the UK, top bosses' pay has grown 20 times faster than that of the average worker, while people in the poorest neighbourhoods in England die seven years younger than those in the richest. When 91-year-old

Why we need to win the fight against inequality

RAF veteran Harry Smith reflected on seeing Britain's increasing 'payday loan sharks, food banks, [and] housing shortages', he recalled his experience of the Great Depression of the 1930s and remarked 'it's not shock I feel but a sense of recognition.' It was once imagined that when a country passes a particular economic stage, its people are freed from poverty. We can now see that they are not. Growth without tackling inequality cannot end poverty.

Inequality hampers growth. The data shows that more equal countries grow more, for longer. This is because a broader consumer base, broader human capital, and the social stability that greater equality enables, together provide a stronger basis for growth than concentrated wealth does; and because tempering wealth concentration mutes asset price cycles and so helps limit economic crashes. Even publications like the *Financial Times* and the *Economist* have noted this, including the great *FT* headline 'Robin Hood's economy: helping the poor boosts growth' and the *Economist* headline 'Up to a point, redistributing income to fight inequality can lift growth'.

Inequality harms opportunity too. When people say 'it doesn't matter how unequal a country is, as long as people have an equal opportunity to make it to the top', they've probably been watching too many Hollywood movies, because they are not describing any real country. The evidence shows that it is much less common for people to make it 'from the bottom to the top' in countries where the gap is widest. As the richest pull away, the ladder falls and breaks. In the US they speak of 'The American Dream'. But where is the American dream most true? Denmark. As Danish multimillionaire entrepreneur Djaffar Shalchi told me, 'I'm not a self-made man, the welfare state made me!' You cannot have extreme inequality and strong social mobility.

As these illustrations demonstrate, even on the narrow terms on which much of the mainstream poverty and economy debates takes place, rising inequality can be seen to be a public bad. When we take a more human and holistic view of the decent society, the damage wrought by inequality can be seen to be even more extensive. Healthy, liveable societies depend on government action to limit inequality: 'In physical health, mental health, drug abuse, education, imprisonment, obesity, social mobility, trust and community life, violence, teenage pregnancies, and child well-being, outcomes are significantly worse in more unequal countries', note Wilkinson and Pickett. Billionaire George Soros describes today's capitalism as 'market fundamentalism' and calls for a return to a more balanced, more managed economy, for all of our futures.

As inequality is intersectional and all forms of inequality influence each other, the intensification of the concentration of wealth of the past few decades has exacerbated inequalities of race and gender. Women, especially women of colour, are the hardest hit by rising economic inequality: they are the workers in the most precarious employment; they suffer the most from cuts in public services; and much of their work, paid and unpaid, is not recognized and rewarded. The wealth gap is highly racialized: median wealth of white Americans is $100,000 while the median wealth of black Americans is less than $10,000 – and increasing inequality is set to widen this gap. Structural discrimination and the concentrated power of the one per cent are inseparable.

Why we need to win the fight against inequality

As we face the climate threat, inequality obstructs tackling it. Just as it is said of 'failed states' that you can only understand them if you understand who is doing well out of the so-called failure, the same is true of 'failed global politics'. Politicians who second-guess scientists are not being stupid – look at their donors, and you'll find many of them are being very clever, just like the 'sceptical' think tankers paid for from oil tankers. Climate change is impossible to make sense of as a debate, precisely *because* it is not a debate; it's a struggle. The broken-down Warsaw negotiations sponsored by the coal industry were a huge success for the sponsors; likewise, the US withdrawal from the Paris accords is not a mistake, but the unfolding of a very intentional plan developed on behalf of companies holding billions. The logic of science is not being followed because it is outweighed by the logic of the concentration of wealth and power. In successfully ensuring a recurring 'not yet' to any moves to tackle climate change, the fossil fuel lobby makes the tobacco industry look like amateurs. At the Paris climate talks, Friends of the Earth chair Jagoda Munić explained to me why environmentalists have concluded that they *have to* confront inequality: 'We cannot bring the changes, on the scale we seek, without a shift of power; our work is to increase the power of communities and to decrease the power of big corporations.'

Inequality is dangerous. It harms security and stability. You can plot on a graph inequality and the percentage of people working as guard labour – the more unequal a society, the more people work as guards. Inequality correlates with the violent crime rate, murder rate, and risk of political violence. A high-powered strategy firm

19

I went to see, PA Consultancy, which advises countries and companies on how to deal with major risks, showed me a copy of the shocking report they'd shared with their clients about the danger of rising inequality. As they noted to their clients, they were not making a moral point; they were making a safety point.

The concentration of wealth enables impunity. After the 2008 financial crisis, in a marked change from earlier financial crises, none of the Wall Street financiers were imprisoned. Across the world, oligarchs and mega-corporations are undermining the culture of the rule of law. Witness the similarities between the way that Glencore avoids paying fair tax in Zambia and the way that Amazon and Google avoid paying their fair share to countries in Europe.

Inequality widens mistrust in society. As the unofficial house journal of the US policy elite *Foreign Affairs* magazine noted: 'The fight over Brexit is a reflection of the social exclusion that arises in a world of stark economic inequality.' Looking at Brexit not as a one-off in one country but as part of a pattern, we see that the broken economic model that breaks societies is starting to break politics.

Organizations that blame society's problems on an Other (their race, ethnicity, religion or sexuality) have grown dramatically – either gaining power or becoming a key political challenge that shifts the mainstream discourse of those in power. Refugees are openly being denied safe haven; ethnic and religious minorities are facing officially sanctioned discrimination; and women are facing an aggressive onslaught of misogyny. Civil society leaders supporting marginalized people are seeing an upsurge of these injustices on every continent.

Why we need to win the fight against inequality

To tackle the forces of intolerance we must also confront the ever-widening inequality that is driving societies apart. Progressive values are put under massive strain when economies cast millions aside. We know from history that the economics of 1929 was a causal factor in the politics of 1933, and that the loss of hope can provide fascists an opportunity to ascend.

The social breakdown caused by inequality can even lead to war. 'Why did the war begin?', explained an academic and activist to me in Colombia, 'Because of inequality. Because the land was taken. Because the farmers had no hope. Unless the causes of the conflict are addressed it will again.' To avoid conflict, economies must be reoriented to create decent jobs, and not see wealth ever more concentrated in the hands of a few.

Perhaps the most profound impact of rising inequality is the danger that instead of reshaping an economic imbalance to ethics and values, we risk allowing ethics and values to be reshaped by economic imbalance. As Martin Luther King warned, we risk substituting 'an "I-it" relationship for the "I-thou" relationship", and relegating persons to the status of things.' Inequality can warp the recognition that all are part of one society, and are, as moral philosopher Jeremy Waldron entitled his book, *One Another's Equals*. As he puts it:

> Massive economic inequality may undermine our adherence to fundamental principles of equal worth and equal dignity. The fact of economic inequality may come to be written in the visible lives of those who are most deprived. It is possible that the principle of basic equality may become less and less credible to us because

21

we become less and less able to imagine what it would be like to live with *these* others on genuinely equal terms. We might become so accustomed to economic inequality, so inured to the spectacle of it despite its being unjustified, that we cease to recognize those who are deprived as nevertheless our equals. It may even be morally embarrassing for us to recognize them as such, since we would then have to acknowledge the injustice. Better perhaps to turn away.

And just as some people stuck at the bottom of the wealth scale have come to be unpeopled and treated as lesser beings, so society has come to ascribe super-human qualities to those at the very top. The Roman Emperor Titus Flavius Vespasianus said, as he died, 'oh dear, I think I am becoming a god'. Now it seems to happen to the richest people while they are still alive. In the words of the great (and much misremembered) Adam Smith, 'this disposition to admire, and almost to worship, the rich and the powerful, and to despise, or, at least, to neglect persons of poor and mean condition, is the great and most universal cause of the corruption of our moral sentiments.'

At the heart of inequality is the cycle of wealth and power. In the phrase that grassroots civil society activists in Pakistan taught me, 'the wealthy get powerful and the powerful get wealthy'. Some people have so much money they don't just buy boats, they buy elections. *This* is what President Roosevelt meant by the 'tyranny of plutocracy'.

Journal: The mining indaba and the protesters

They call it an 'indaba' – a word in several African languages for a gathering where a community gets together to resolve the problems that affect them all. But it is no community meeting – it is the world's largest meeting of the mining industry, where the rich and powerful from across the world gather in a plush Cape Town conference centre to determine where will be mined and who will get the money. It is a meeting, in its own words, 'dedicated to the capitalization and development of mining interests in Africa', at which 'a powerful group ... make the vital relationships to sustain their investment interests'. In the front rooms the delegates are entertained by Goldman Sachs, Dambisa Moyo and Tony Blair. In the back rooms mining corporations meet to cut secret deals with friendly governments and pressure any governments who have started making trouble.

Through the huge glass windows the delegates can see protests. But they don't get to hear what the protesters have to say. They dismiss them as anti-mining, anti-progress. It is easy to complain, argue the mining indaba attendees, but would you really want an end to all mining? No, say campaigners, who gathered in much less comfortable surroundings a few miles away for an 'alternative indaba'. When I get to hear the stories of some of the participants of the alternative indaba, I get to understand that theirs is not a case 'against mining' but for accountability. The problem they highlight is not the existence of mining but a harmful imbalance of power that renders mining corporations a law unto themselves. Here's what I heard from activists from across Africa:

> The sharing agreements on mining deals in our country are secret. So we the public don't know what our national wealth has been sold for. After pressure, permission was given to MPs to view these long and complicated agreements in a specific room for a set period of time without taking notes, so we're starting to get a picture, but we can't get final confirmation. From what we're seeing it looks like a really bad deal indeed – which is why it is secret in the first place.

> Our laws require that a set percentage of the proceeds must go to the community, yet we find places where the mining company has now finished and left, the environment has been trashed, and the community's share was never provided.

> Many of our officials and ministers and their family members are private shareholders or on the pay of the mining corporations, officially or unofficially, so when we challenge the corporations we are challenging the government.

> The fines for mining companies who break the laws are so low that the mining corporations happily factor them in as a cost of business.

> When we revealed illegal water pollution by a diamond mine, it was not the mining corporation who were arrested, but us.

Our government is finally standing up to mining corporations and demanding they pay their fair share of tax. But neighbouring governments have shown absolutely no solidarity. The AU [African Union] has to work much more closely together. We cannot have a race to the bottom.

When you start to engage the mining corporations you hope to change them, but if you are not careful they can end up changing you. After we criticized a mining corporation, they invited us for a tour so, they said, we could see that they were not as we had said. At the end of the tour they tried to present us with gems 'as a souvenir gift'. We told them we were not allowed to accept hospitality. The message was clear.

Campaigners are asking governments to hold mining corporations to account to ensure open, transparent agreements so citizens know what is happening with their national wealth; a fair share of tax revenue; free, prior and informed consent, so that acquiring communities' land requires that communities agree; fair wages, protection of workers' health and safety and workers' rights to organize; and adherence to environmental laws. They are demanding, too, that mining corporations stop lobbying for a lowering of these basic standards.

What should bring prosperity is instead bringing misery. Legitimate challenge to the mining industry is being met not with answers but with brute force of the entitled one per cent. Governments, who should be overseeing corporations and protecting citizens, are instead protecting corporations and overseeing citizens. The proposals put forward by the mining industry's critics do not constitute an end to mining but an insistence on real democracy. They are reminding communities that 'what's mined is yours'. Which is exactly why the mining industry is so determined to keep them down.

This is not about some people having more things, notes Chuck Collins; it is about 'the power to rig the rules of our economy and shape the culture through ownership of media'. In polls, majorities in the 60-and-70-something-per cents across a wide range of countries say that the rich have too much influence. Superb recent books like *Dark Money* and *Affluence and Influence* confirm that this sense is accurate. Inequality promotes what political scientists have dubbed 'social capture'. Economist Jeff Sachs explains how it works: 'Corporations write the rules and pay the politicians, sometimes illegally and sometimes via ways that are called legal, financing their campaigns or massive lobbying. This has got completely out of control and is leading to the breakdown of modern democracy.'

In this way, what makes inequality distinct from the other policy issues and social challenges we face is that inequality is the *meta-issue*, because it represents not one decision to be made but the question of how *all* decisions are made, and *who* gets to make them. We cannot say 'sure, inequality is important but let's first address these other issues', because inequality – that is, the massive imbalance of power caused by the extreme concentration of wealth – *prevents* those issues from being properly addressed.

Anti-apartheid leader Jay Naidoo has declared the widening chasm across the world between a powerful few and the rest to be 'Apartheid 2.0'. As five major NGO leaders set out in a joint call to action, 'the widening gap and imbalance of power between the richest and the rest is warping the rules and policies that affect all of us in society, creating a vicious circle of ever growing and harmful undue influence.' Privilege and wealth are reshaping economic and social systems at the expense of people as a whole and the planet.

How we won the debate

For several decades until very recently, elite institutions and governments showed considerable hostility to the suggestion that they should address inequality. Inequality had been the great blind spot of the internationally agreed Millennium Development Goals (MDGs) for the period 2000–15. Even when countries formally achieved the MDG targets, they often did so in a way that left behind the poorest people.

When the new goals for the period 2015–30, the Sustainable Development Goals (SDGs), were being negotiated, civil society pressed that these needed to include a specific goal on inequality. But the proposal published by the so-called High-Level Panel, the initial intergovernmental drafting group on what should be included in the SDGs, excluded a goal on inequality. When civil society groups challenged them on that omission, senior government officials contacted organizations to express their anger at the impudence and warn of consequences for organizations which criticized them – I was the subject of one of those aggressive phone calls.

Regulators warned anti-poverty organizations that they had no mandate to address inequality. Mainstream economists were reluctant to come out against inequality. Even within NGOs, it was challenging to secure backing for calls to reduce inequality. (I remember how at one NGO I was working in, there was a report for which it was hard to get internal sign off. Fortunately, we had sent a copy to the Chief Economist of the Bank of England and he'd written back saying it was great. So I carried that letter in my jacket pocket all the time. That way, I was able to produce it for anyone in the NGO who said we might not be able to sign off the report, as it would be tricky for any colleagues to say that the Chief Economist of the Bank of England didn't understand economics or was too radical!)

Criticizing inequality was deemed too 'political', 'anti-rich' and 'unrealistic'. We were told that rising inequality was necessary for growth and progress, or that it was irrelevant to tackling poverty, or that technology made it inevitable. We were told that governments would never accept the call to tackle inequality.

But in a surprisingly short time the taboo started to break. Institutions who had once rejected it began to formally recognize it. The output of the IMF research department epitomized this intellectual shift.

Journal: The IMF research department slams inequality

The IMF paper, 'Macro-Structural Policies and Income Inequality in Low-Income Developing Countries', was one in a series that marked the intellectual journey the IMF research department has travelled in recent years.

This particular paper was especially notable because it recognized that tackling inequality required key progressive policies and increased public spending – i.e. the opposite of the budget cuts that it once advocated. In IMF style, they even created a formula – a 1 per cent increase in public spending, they reported, led to a 2.3 per cent decrease in inequality after 5 years! It also took a strong stand against prioritizing indirect taxes, such as VAT, showing that they increase inequality. It helped strengthen the evidence base around the kinds of policies necessary to reduce inequality, including several that civil society organizations had been raising, including direct taxes over indirect taxes, boosting investment in social services, expanding cash transfer programmes, and offsetting anything likely to increase inequality with measures to decrease inequality.

Packed with detailed quantitative analysis, it demonstrated that much of what elites had been advancing as unquestioned economics was demonstrably harmful both to economic growth and to public well-being. What made these IMF papers surprising was also what makes them so powerful: an institution that had been, for far too long, a defender of the free market story and the Washington Consensus – liberalizing trade, privatizing everything possible and cutting down public spending – had now very publicly refuted it. We could now include the IMF among those who had comprehensively set out why the broken economics that dominated four decades must be consigned to the dustbin of history.

The final negotiations for the UN's SDGs marked a turning point. After the High-Level Panel's first draft of the international Sustainable Development Goals had excluded a goal on inequality, it had seemed a very tough prospect to turn that position around. Well-intentioned insiders warned campaigners to concentrate instead on trying to preserve what was there, claiming that the final is *never* more ambitious than the draft. But civil society held the line, and leading economists, UN officials and key national representatives endorsed their call. Then the UN Sustainable Development Goals negotiations shifted, and in September 2015 every single world leader signed up to 'reduce inequality within and between countries'. The aim to get political leaders to agree to reduce inequality – once dismissed as the height of unrealism by the insider-advocacy crowd – was won in the clearest, most irrefutable way possible.

World leaders started repeatedly emphasizing their determination to reverse rising inequality. The words we never thought they'd say turned from a trickle into a mighty river. A commitment to reduce inequality, which governments had rejected for decades, became the cornerstone of official policy discourse. The South African government pledged a priority focus on tackling inequality. The European Union declared reducing inequality key to its own and global harmony. Nigeria's outgoing Finance Minister, the veteran World Bank and market economy icon Ngozi Okonjo-Iweala, declared that Nigeria's challenge is the divide between 'the 99.9% and a venal, kleptocratic, power-hungry elite that have colonized the country and refuse to let go' – in an interview in the *FT*! French President Macron declared at his inauguration that social division has driven extremism, and that to heal the divisions the government must fight inequality. The G7 joined in, too.

Even Wall Street acknowledged it. 'The current level of income inequality', noted ratings agency S&P, 'is dampening economic growth, and the last generation's inequality will extend into the next generation, with diminished social mobility. Rebalancing – along with spending in the areas of education, health care, and infrastructure – could help bring under control an income gap that, at its current level, threatens the stability of an economy still struggling to recover.' Goldman Sachs CEO Lloyd Blankfein remarked that 'inequality is destabilizing, inequality is responsible for our divisions, and the divisions could get wider.'

Economics dumped the old religion. What had been heresy became orthodoxy: it was now accepted that inequality harmed economic and social progress and had got out of hand. As the World Social Science Report noted, there was a 'five-fold increase in studies of inequality and social justice in academic publications' from 1992 to 2016. The argument that inequality was now excessive and was socially, politically and economically corrosive – once dismissed as Soviet romanticism – was now accepted by pretty much a clean sweep of establishment institutions. As the UN University summarized the new consensus: 'The level of inequality in the world is far beyond what any economic argument can justify.'

Those few denialists still publicly defending inequality looked a sorry rump, reminiscent of the Afrikaner 'Bittereinders' or the Japanese soldier found still fighting the Second World War in a Philippines jungle decades after it was over. With the debate won, now would come the action, or so we imagined.

Journal: Will no one defend the tax dodgers?

World leaders' rhetoric has been getting tougher and tougher on tax dodgers. First, the African Union's Heads of State unanimously accepted all the recommendations of the High-Level Panel on Illicit Financial Flows, headed by Thabo Mbeki, which was outspoken in declaring multinational corporations as the big offenders. Then, in Britain, the head of the National Crime Agency declared war on the 'hundreds of billions of pounds of criminal money laundered through UK banks', and, in the US, politicians promised to tackle 'corporate deserters'. Newspaper stories created a worldwide drumbeat of shame.

With this new mainstream, most corporations have gone out of their way to distance themselves from the label of 'tax dodger'. They have stressed their respect for the law, their recognition of the importance of taxation. Their social licence to operate demanded that they promise that they were on the side of the public.

In this context, the Adam Smith Institute's outspoken support for tax avoidance has been a valuable reminder that progress on tackling tax avoidance is difficult not only, or even primarily, because it is technically complex, but because some people believe that tax avoidance is just fine. In the words of the Adam Smith Institute, which once played a very influential role in economic policy, 'advising people on how to avoid certain corporate taxes in poorer African countries' shows 'public spiritedness' and is 'a bloody good idea': 'If you've advised people to dodge that corporate taxation', they add, 'you've just raised the wages of some of the poorest people in the world.'

With all due respect to the Adam Smith Institute for not hiding their teeth on this one, and with somewhat less respect for their mis-remembering of the historical Adam Smith, they are not our prime opponent.

Our prime opponents are much sneakier, much cleverer, than the outspoken ideologues who publicly declare that dodging is good. The people we have to fear operate not in the light but in the shadows. They say that they support reforms to tackle tax dodging, just not the ones we propose, or they say they support the ones we propose, and then flood Washington, Brussels, London and the world's poorest countries with lobbyists hired to undermine progress. Of course, most of what the big corporations do to avoid tax is legal. They spend a fortune on lobbying to ensure it stays that way.

We've won the argument on tax. But that's just phase one in the long struggle for tax justice. Our opponents are hugely rich, frighteningly powerful and totally unscrupulous, and are not used to losing. Goliath has been shamed, but he's still massive. We have not reached the end of the war on tax dodging. We've not even reached the beginning of the end. But, we have, at least, reached the end of the beginning.

Why winning the debate is not enough and we have to win the fight

To have governments across the world admit the inequality crisis, and agree to tackle it, was once seen as an overly ambitious advocacy goal. It was surpassed, far better, far faster, than we had hoped. We had to pinch ourselves to check that it was not all just a dream. It was a moment to savour.

But now in the cold light of day we can see to what extent this has had a real-world impact. It is clear that when all is said and done, much more has been said than done. We are feasting on promises and fasting on delivery. As economist Andy Sumner summed it up to me: 'There has been a big increase in decision makers' noise about inequality but surprisingly little action in terms of real structural change.'

Leaders have started to talk our language, but what we need isn't nicer language; it's a fairer society. We can be pleased that the international financial institutions now acknowledge that inequality has become out of control and needs to be tackled. But they haven't yet shifted how they actually operate in countries. The World Bank's continued complicity with school fees is still hindering access to free education for all. The IMF still promotes austerity and regressive taxes, generating crises in countries from Jordan to Chile.

We can be pleased that every government committed at the UN to reduce inequality within and between countries – something that very senior leaders from very powerful countries told many of us they would never ever commit to, just weeks before they did. But there are still very few countries in which inequality is being substantially reduced – and progress to reducing inequality *between* countries continues to be undermined by rich countries blocking progress on tackling tax dodging, reforming trade and tackling the climate crisis. Central banks and Finance Ministries *talk* of having learnt their lesson about inequality from the 2008 financial crisis, but, economist Richard Murphy warned me, 'their practice remains much as it was and right now feels like 1929.'

The contrast between promises and delivery on inequality is perhaps best illustrated by Davos, the annual gathering of corporate and political elites on a Swiss mountain for the World Economic Forum (WEF).

Why we need to win the fight against inequality

The WEF has continued to list inequality as one of the world's major challenges. Every year it pledges action. But its actual record in reducing inequality has been summarized by Branko Milanović as having 'produced 0 results'. As a *Financial Times* editor noted in a diary tweet from the mountain, which best captured the spirit: 'Unsurprised that biz figures in Davos are saying ... [high marginal rates on the super-rich] would be dangerous to growth, which is a) nonsense and b) drives home that they continue to prioritise outsized personal gains over fairness & stability'.

The Davos Men are not only at the peak of the mountain and at the peak of any graph of wealth; they are also at the peak of their collective power: the super-rich are determining the parameters of what governments do. Davos can never be the answer, because the problem is caused by the influence of the people at Davos.

For students of history, none of this should be at all surprising: never, at any time or place, have great strides been made in tackling the concentration of power and wealth in the hands of a few by literally concentrating together those powerful and wealthy few. As the gospels teach us, if we are to exalt the humbled, we will have to humble the exalted.

It's important to emphasize that the issue is *not* the personal moral character of the individual members of the one per cent. Indeed, far too much time is lost, when we could be organizing, by first trying to work out if people in power in oppressive systems are personally irredeemably not nice – as if that is what determines whether or not we need to organize. Even the nicest ones won't give us a more equal society – it will only be won by the rest of us pushing for it together. As Aimé Césaire advised about colonialists: 'Do not seek to know whether personally these gentlemen are in good or bad faith, whether personally they have good or bad intentions. Whether personally – that is in the private conscience of Peter.' What matters is the *imbalance of* power: without fixing that, we cannot fix the injustice.

Just as a strategy to reduce inequality cannot rely on the generosity of the super-rich, so too it cannot rely on the courage of political leaders. Consider a political leader prospering politically from the status quo. He (for it is most likely a *he*) sees that there is huge public concern about rising inequality, and that demands for a redistribution of power and wealth from the one per cent to the rest have suddenly again become mainstream. What is he to do? If he rejects those demands, he risks legitimacy. But if he acts on them, the plutocrats will work to see to it that he falls. The best way forward, for the cynical leader, or the scared one, or the dull one, is to agree to act and then do nothing meaningful about it. Gandhi said about those in power: 'First they ignore you, then they laugh at you, then they fight you, then you win.' Perhaps Gandhi should have said: 'Then *they tell you* that you have won, and then, only if you keep pushing, can you really win.'

Now, let us imagine instead a political leader who really *does* want to tackle inequality. She tries to pass a series of measures redistributing from those at the top; and so, in turn, some of those at the top, very rationally, spend a fortune (but still a fraction of what those measures would cost them) on cajoling, threatening, tempting and undermining her and everyone around her, and on spreading a message that the proposed measures will fail, break the country, and hurt the poor hardest. *Without* a strong movement from below, the lone good politician, even if she does not buckle, will see her solo work stopped and broken. Even with the best political leaders, the fight against inequality cannot be won unless ordinary people organize and take on the power of those at the top.

Likewise, because inequality is not just a policy issue but a power one, the work of providing comprehensive analyses about the damage of inequality and detailing policy solutions, useful though it is, won't on its own bring change. Elites are not waiting to be better informed by civil society before they voluntarily make things fairer. For as long as any group has a monopoly of power they will never 'give' justice – it has to be won by building a countervailing power. The imbalance between *those at the very top* and the rest of us means that to lift up the 'have-nots' then we'll need to let down the 'have-yachts'.

Audre Lorde described the task of those fighting inequality as 'learning how to make common cause with those others identified as outside the structures, in order to define and seek a world in which we can all flourish … For the master's tools will never dismantle the master's house.' It is not through business as usual that we will transform business as usual.

The aim cannot be simply to get the privileged to be gentler; it must be to get them less privileged. Inequality *can* be overcome – but only if we *fight* it.

How we won the fight against inequality before

Why looking back can help us plan forward
When the region most hit by inequality became the
    region leading progress to turn it around
When people's organizing secured an international
    'Golden Age'
When the forces for inequality inflicted our biggest
    defeat, and what we can learn from our opponents
Learning from history in the fight against inequality

Why looking back can help us plan forward

Understanding the past is key to building a more equal
future. When I met with Tarana Burke, founder of
the #MeToo movement, she explained to me the first
thing she advises people who want to bring change is
'read history!' Because we have won the fight against
inequality before, we know that we can win it again,
and learning how we have won the fight before can help
guide us to future victories.

Let's begin our look at history with another quiz. It's
a question that was asked at Davos by an American

billionaire when he was asked if he'd support a high marginal tax rate on the super-rich. 'Can you name a country where that's worked, ever?' Well, can anyone?

Embarrassingly for the American billionaire, his fellow panellist could. The answer is the United States! As was pointed out, from the 1930s to the 1960s the US marginal tax rate on the super-rich ranged from 70 per cent to nearly 95 per cent, 'and those were pretty good years for growth' (and for a growth that working people shared in). This high rate of tax on the super-rich, and relatively high investment in public services to benefit ordinary people, was maintained in this period under both Democrat and Republican Presidents. It was the accepted, expected, norm.

History shows that extreme or ever-rising inequality is not inevitable. While there has never been a moment when everyone had the exact same wealth and power, we have had sustained periods when inequality has gone on a significant downward trajectory. We should view these as victories for two reasons. The first is that for as long as inequality is going significantly downwards, you are winning. The second is that such periods guided societies to an understanding that people are of equal value – something that depends on the enabling of a shared experience and the levelling of power imbalances that tackling inequality brings. As the great Uruguayan writer Eduardo Galeano so beautifully remarked: 'Utopia lies at the horizon. When I draw nearer by two steps, it retreats two steps. If I proceed ten steps forward, it swiftly slips ten steps ahead. No matter how far I go, I can never reach it. What, then, is the purpose of utopia? It is to cause us to advance.'

So, when inequality has been beaten before, how has it been done? In a brilliantly written but depressing book, *The Great Leveler*, the historian Walter Scheidel implies that beating inequality requires a catastrophe. His argument looks in particular at the contribution of the legacy of the Second World War in the development of more egalitarian societies to conclude that only events like the Second World War can overcome inequality (other cheerful examples include England's 'Black Death' plague that killed so many ordinary people that the remaining ones had better bargaining power in the labour market!).

Yet, while it is true that such catastrophes are an important part of the history of authorities facing up to inequality, catastrophes are not only awful in themselves but are very unreliable handmaidens of progress. (There is no reason to conclude, for example, that the fall-out from the Covid-19 epidemic will by itself lead us through choppy waters to better times.) Rather, history shows that progress in tackling inequality has been won through people's own collective struggle. Alone, we may indeed be trapped by the structures in which we find ourselves, but by acting together, we have the capacity to remake them, as we'll see illustrated in this chapter.

None of this is to say that winning the fight against inequality is easy – only that it is possible, because it has been done before. In the words of Noam Chomsky: 'If you assume that there is no hope, you guarantee that there will be no hope. If you assume that there are opportunities to change things, then there is a possibility that you can contribute to making a better world.'

How we won the fight against inequality before

To uncover the patterns of what works in winning the fight against inequality, let us look at two key episodes of inequality reduction: the turning of the tide in Latin America in the 2000s, and the 'Golden Age' in several regions of the world in the long mid-twentieth century.

When the region most hit by inequality became the region leading progress to turn it around

One of the most important recent examples of significant progress in reducing inequality was in Latin America in the period from roughly 2000 for a decade or a decade and a half. Each country's experience was different, of course, but some important shared trends connected a range of Latin American countries in this period that saw the continent with the worst inequality become a beacon for how to tackle it.

In a context of Brazil being one of the most unequal countries in the world, for example, real progress on tackling inequality was made: as the World Social Science Report noted, 'the incomes of the poorest Brazilians [rose] more than five times faster than those of the richest, women's incomes faster than men's, black people's faster than whites', the impoverished northeast faster than the rich south-east'. The incomes of the richest still kept advancing, but the incomes of the poor rose more quickly. In Bolivia, even more progress against inequality was made, even faster. As these examples show, spiralling inequality is not fate: governments can choose to take the steps which reduce inequality.

Beating inequality depends on appropriate action by government. On one level, therefore, we can accurately say that inequality was reduced in Latin America because from around the year 2000 a set of governments decided to address it, and implemented some of the policy mix needed to reduce inequality. They redistributed some land from large landholders to landless people; they increased the wages of the poorest people by increasing the legal minimum, strengthening labour law enforcement, and enabling trade union representation; they increased social protection for children and the elderly; they expanded public services like health and education, paid for with progressive taxes; they organized economic policy around jobs; and they tackled discrimination.

But when we look at the deeper causes of that success in tackling inequality, we can't start in 2000, we need to look earlier, and we can't *start* with the decisions that were made by those governments, as the more interesting question is *why*? Why, in a region so unequal, where for decades before, governments had pursued policies which exacerbated inequality, did the governments of the 2000s act differently? The short answer is because ordinary people built up their collective power, and it was this power which successfully pressured *and enabled* those governments to act.

From landless workers' movements in Brazil to indigenous people's movements in Bolivia, organizing from below was the key to securing change. As political scientist Leandro Vergara-Camus notes, 'the most progressive policies of the Partido dos Trabalhadores (PT) government under Lula in Brasil were a response to decades of activism.' The International Inequalities Institute at the London School of Economics was likewise able to trace how the pursuit of policies to reduce inequality across Latin America was 'driven by local social movements for change'. Oxford University's Diego Sánchez-Ancochea, one of the leading experts of this period, titled one of his papers 'It's the politics, stupid!' And, as he explained to me, by politics he does not only mean party contestation, but the social movements which both generate parties and pressure them – this pressure is vital because without it there is no counter to the permanent pressure from elites.

Journal: 'Organized we are powerful' – lessons from the Brazilian land rights movement

'This dance is not mine alone, this dance is by us all' – the women move as one circle, hand in hand. Then, still as one circle, they put their arms around each other – 'when we are tired, we have each other's shoulders to rest on.'

The women, members of an organization of coconut pickers from the forest region in Maranhão state in north-east Brazil, proudly show us the fruits of their labour: coconuts turned into oil, soap, flour and more; a cooperative factory that processes the goods so that they don't need to rely on middlemen; a small farm with a vegetable patch, a fishpond and a chicken coop. And they talk of the victories won in the face of entrenched power.

The richest man in this area claimed that all this land was his. He was also the area's politician.

> He had the money power and the political power.
> The family have been powerful for hundreds of
> years. Police and gunmen kept harassing us. They
> told us to leave but we had nowhere else to go. I
> remember the sound of the six bullets.

But they do not want to dwell on the pain. When a
conversation turns to those who died, one woman
interjects 'but if we keep on telling all these sad
stories we could go on for days. What do we need
to do now?'

Their organizing secured real progress: those
landless workers who collect coconuts from
the forests and from the big estates successfully
campaigned for a law that protects their right to
do so; some communities have secured recognition
for the small pieces of land on which they live
and farm; the cooperatives have secured from the
government a guaranteed minimum price for key
products so that they can be assured of a minimum
income; in several districts the groups have secured
free, public, pre-school for small children and won
access to water and sanitation.

All are clear how these victories were won.
'Individually we coconut-breakers are small. But
when we organized, we became visible. We said,
"look at us, listen."' 'Everything we have achieved
has been through the strength of our friendship.'
'We got together in our community, then we
linked with communities across the region. We
went and got support from the trade unions, from
the Catholic Church, and from the wider public.

We started an association and kept pressing for our rights to earn a living and live in dignity.'

They are clear that they cannot rely on the goodwill of politicians. When the local establishment politician was replaced by his daughter, 'it made no difference that she was a woman. She was her father's daughter. He lived on through her.'

There is a recognition that the national government of Lula, whose party emerged from the social movements and which brought several leaders of the social movement into power, introduced substantial reforms and was the best government they have known. Unemployment was reduced, the minimum wage increased, and inequality went down. But, they say, 'we made a mistake of thinking when the good people got into power, we didn't need to keep pressuring them. It's like we went to sleep. Whoever is in power we need to keep pushing.' 'Yes', says a coconut breaker, 'things are better, but now, when we try to enter the coconut forests to which we have the right of access, the big landlords, who used to kill us with dogs and guns, kill us with electric fences instead.' 'Yes', agrees a peasant farmer, 'we have managed to stay on our farm, but we are still denied water. We want more than to live, we want to live with dignity.'

There is a worry that the Dilma government [in power at the time], which pledged to continue the progress of Lula has instead, under pressure from big corporations and landlords, started to roll back. 'They have stopped listening to us. Government listens to the rich and big companies. Not to us, the poor, Indians, blacks, women. We have to struggle.'

They share, none the less, a profound sense that their struggle will ultimately win. Discussions regularly burst into song. 'Even though it is dark, I sing, for the morning will come.' In one community facing eviction, we meet in the one-room clay and straw building they built as their church, their school, the headquarters of their association, and their village meeting hall. They call the building 'Our Lady of Good Hope.'

'We are strong. My grandfather escaped from slavery with his friends. And I have secured my piece of land with you, my friends. But we cannot just wait. We need to demand.'

At a special event of the landless movements, Deje, a coconut breaker, is seated next to a government official who apologizes for having arrived late and for needing to leave early. Deje stands up and directly addresses him in front of the crowd. Brazilian Portuguese has such a sweet melody that to the English ear everything I've heard, whatever the content, has sounded gentle. Until now. She points her finger at his face. 'Whenever we try to meet government, they fail to see us. Whenever we write to government they fail to reply.' She pulls out a piece a paper. 'We have a letter for you. I'm going to read it to you.'

It begins: 'We landless demand our right to fetch coconuts unharassed by landowners...' Then the coup de grace: 'Now, you cannot leave until you sign it. We need you to sign it right now.' And he does. Then he thanks her. 'We know that all progress depends on the social movements. We need to work with you.' We've just witnessed a lesson in courage, in democracy, and in power. It is the same lesson we learnt in the dance. And that we read on the T-shirt of one of the landless women workers: 'Organizadas Somos Fortes' – Organized we are powerful.

It should be noted that the progress in tackling inequality in Latin America did not get it all right, and that it was limited and has since suffered a swing back, because of two significant flaws. One flaw was that progressive Latin American governments did not pursue as fully as they should have undoing the vastly outsized accumulation of wealth of the very richest, which meant that often just a few well-known families continued to have wealth exceeding the total assets of whole sections of the population. Because it was, mostly, kept intact, the power of that group to organize a counter-reaction was not sufficiently addressed – and when the counter-reaction did come, many progressive policies could swiftly be undone. The key lesson here is that wealth is not merely a number, but a form of power – and that tackling inequality means needing to be bold in tackling that power, addressing the structural roots and not only the consequences of inequality.

A second flaw that increased the vulnerability of the progress in Latin America was the lack of sufficient challenge from below during the period of progressive government. This was in part because good people assumed that having 'our leaders' in power meant that challenge was consequently no longer necessary or was even unhelpful – but such a view keeps being rebutted by history, as it was again. Because the pressures from those at the top never cease, a lack of strong challenge from below led to progressive governments pursuing regressive measures and getting too close to plutocrats, thus weakening accountability, feeding cynicism, and ultimately facilitating the return of regressive elites to power.

The lesson here is that the pressure from below is not needed at one moment but ongoing, indeed forever, *whoever* is 'in power'. As activist Pedro Telles explained to me,

> when the 2000s saw a wave of strong leaders in government committed to fighting inequality, too many of us civil society organizations stopped grassroots organizing. Some of us went into government. Many had close contacts in government and focused our energies and time there – but having dropped the grass-roots organizing, when politics and politicians changed, it was hard to get that back. Now we have to get back to basics, and so we are learning again how to do it, building relations between activists across organizations as people with a common mission rather than as organizational representatives negotiating for their part.

Of course, these mistakes should not lead us to be disheartened but instead to regroup. And that is beginning. Latin America showed that by building from

How we won the fight against inequality before

the grassroots – indeed, only by building from the grassroots – inequality could be reduced, in our time. That
shows that we can still win, and it shows how. The fight
back starts at the grassroots, again.

When people's organizing secured an international 'Golden Age'

Internationally, the key story of progress in tackling
inequality has been the long mid-twentieth century.
It's a story that includes North America, Europe and
newly independent nations in Africa and Asia. The
transformation in so many parts of the world was so
significant that the last thirty years of the period (from
the mid-1940s to the mid-1970s) came to be known as
the 'Golden Age'. People's organizing was at its heart.
It was an age in some ways epitomized by the award
of the Nobel Peace Prize to the International Labour
Organization (ILO) in 1969, in which the securing of
workers' rights and workers' collective voice was recognized as foundational to social harmony.

Of course, not everything was 'golden' and there
remained many continuing brutal injustices and great
challenges; even the generalization was applicable only
in particular countries; and an exact replication of all
of its aspects cannot be our model for the future. But
it is a powerful example of what is possible on such
a scale in such a range of contexts, and the progress
that people secured, from such a challenging base, can
be an inspiration for us today. As London School of
Economics' Rebecca Simson summarizes it, 'over the
course of the middle half of the twentieth century,

countries around the world underwent dramatic social transformations as incomes grew, inequalities declined and living standards improved.'

It might seem strange to begin telling the Golden Age story in the US, the country which in many ways epitomizes inequality. But that is the point. Even there, substantial progress was made in tackling inequality in that time. And the progress lasted a long time. The big gains started to come to fruition in the 1930s, overcame the Great Depression, and continued until the 1970s: it included the New Deal, the Great Society and the progress made on Civil Rights.

The movements fighting racial inequality and economic inequality are sometimes written about today as if they were two parallel tracks. But, as Jane McAlevey notes in *No Shortcuts*, it is 'impossible to sort the process into two distinct piles or traditions'. Activists at the time were clear, as Martin Luther King put it, that racial and economic injustice were 'inseparable twins' and that the full realization of civil rights required tackling 'the gulf between superfluous wealth and abject poverty' and confronting 'the danger of the profit motive as the sole basis for an economic system'.

The progressive policies enacted in that period in the US came from a combination of pressures from below. It came from trade unions, from black organizations, from churches and from other progressive grassroots groups together devoting their energies, in Dr King's words, 'to organize our strength into compelling power so that government cannot elude our demands.' In the Venn diagram of the movements, you'll see people like the African-American trade union organizer Philip Randolf, who successfully pressured both the FDR and the Kennedy-Johnson governments by reminding them of the power of organized people – without which we would not remember them as such reforming Presidents.

The progress that was made depended on people showing courage to defy authority. And they depended on decades of brave, determined challenge to build the basis for success. For example, the 1909 'Uprising' of thousands of workers striking and protesting in the streets was initiated not by the more senior and established leaders of the unions, but by those at the grassroots like Clara Lemlich who famously declared at a meeting to discuss their plight: 'I am a working girl, one of those who are on strike against intolerable conditions. I am tired of listening to speakers who talk in general terms. What we are here for is to decide whether we shall strike or shall not strike. I offer a resolution that a general strike be declared *now.*' Later, in the 1930s, Lemlich helped coordinate rent strikes to secure rent reductions and boycotts to secure food price reductions; for her boldness she was blacklisted from garment shops, fired from roles in progressive organizations who found her too radical, and faced repeated harassment and repression by government; but without the courage of many determined grassroots leaders like Lemlich there would not have been the build-up of pressure for change.

In the 1960s, in turn, those who took part in sit-ins faced beatings, and those who marched faced dogs and fire hoses. The FBI engaged in what its domestic intelligence division head admitted was a 'no holds barred, rough, tough' operation against civil rights organizers, trade unions and other activists for greater equality, whom it treated as a dangerous threat.

How we won the fight against inequality before

Perhaps most dispiriting for the fight against inequality was that that even many 'allies' publicly condemned those like the civil rights movement who confronted power. As King and others went to jail in 1963 in Birmingham, Alabama for protest, mainstream church leaders issued a statement condemning them for 'demonstrations ... led in part by outsiders ... that are unwise and untimely, ... incite to hatred [and] have not contributed to the resolution of our local problems', and urged the 'community to withdraw support from these demonstrations' and 'not [to go] to the streets [but] observe law and order and common sense.' It was this condemnation that led King to state in his powerful reply that the greatest stumbling block to progress was not the implacable opponent but those who claim to support change but were 'more devoted to order than to justice.' Those fighting inequality had not only to overcome this pressure from others but also to overcome their own internalized 'fear of being nonconformists' and be willing to be not 'merely a thermometer that recorded the ideas and principles of popular opinion [but] a thermostat that transformed the mores of society'.

Determined, laborious and patient organizing bringing together a critical mass of people was also key. The Montgomery bus boycott is sometimes told as if it was only a story of Rosa Parks sitting down and Martin Luther King speaking. But it was planned, and trained for. Rosa Parks wasn't just tired! And as Dr King himself pointed out, 'I neither started the protest nor suggested it, I simply responded to the call of the people for a spokesman'. Fred Gray, the lawyer for the bus boycotters, recalled how it was won: 'they say it takes a village to raise a child; it took the whole of Montgomery's black community to win the fight against segregation in transportation.'

Two years before Rosa Parks was arrested, the Women's Political Leadership Council, a group of African-American activists, had been preparing for a bus boycott. The Montgomery Improvement Association, set up after the arrest, had to maintain the boycott for 381 days. And they had to resource it from the community. Activists printed thousands of flyers to get the message out and got hundreds of volunteers to help organize. Black churches across the city served as centres of organizing. People who didn't even use the bus helped by providing people lifts in their cars. Postal service workers helped work out the routes carpools should take. Taxi operators agreed to reduce rates. The organizers of the boycott had to hold huge numbers of meetings. They had to fend off legal challenges – and violent attacks. But, because of the joined-up organization uniting faith groups, women's groups, labour unions and others, holding together even under strain, they won. As civil rights leader Diane Nash noted, 'It took many thousands of people to make the changes that we made, people whose names we'll never know. They'll never get credit for the sacrifices they've made, but I remember them.'

The movements were successful because they built real power. Advancements in the US on workers' rights, social protection and civil rights all came, as Jane McAlevey notes, from 'powerful movements, led by ordinary people, [who built the] ability to sustain massive disruptions to the existing order'. The impact on inequality of the rise in this period of people joining unions, especially, is so clear that economic historian Colin Gordon has shown how you can even plot it on graphs. And this impact was not only the case at the individual corporation and at sector level, but also, crucially, at the *societal* level. Unionization didn't just make a difference for those unionized workers, or even just in their industries: unionization changed the country. (And just as the rise of unionization was central to the progress made, so too later it was the weakening of unions which was central to bringing about the inequality explosion which followed when the 'Golden Age' was brought to its end.) Cesar Chavez, who organized US farm workers, put it so succinctly and so beautifully: 'We don't need perfect political systems. We need perfect participation.'

When the civil rights movement's 1962 Operation Breadbasket challenged companies to increase the share of profits going to black workers and communities, it was only *after* the movement showed that they could successfully organize a boycott that those companies, in Martin Luther King's words, 'the next day were talking nice, were very humble, and [later] we signed the agreement.' That's why King, when challenged by the so-called 'moderates' who asked why he needed to organize, replied 'we have not made a single gain without determined pressure ... lamentably it is an historical fact that privileged groups seldom give up their privileges voluntarily ... freedom is never voluntarily given by the oppressor, it must be demanded by the oppressed.'

Central to the success too was the effective telling of a story. Social problems, as US civil rights leader

John Lewis pointed out, were moral problems on a larger scale. Those fighting inequality understood that a key challenge they faced was that inequality had been normalized: 'Who hears a clock tick, or the surf murmur, or the train pass?' asked Dr King, 'not those who live by the clock, or the sea, or the track'. That is why the movement put so much effort into ensuring that inequalities were made visible – 'dramatizing a shameful condition' – and why they ensured too that an alternative vision of a mutuality was articulated in such a resonant way.

The union movement understood that workers had been inculcated to see the wealthy as the achievers and to seek social advancement as individuals. So, through slogans and songs, they constructed a new narrative, emphasizing that the great achievements of the country had been the work of ordinary people who therefore deserved to be respected accordingly. And they set out how together, and *only* together, they could ensure that they were treated as they deserved:

All the world that's owned by idle drones is ours and
  ours alone.
We have laid the wide foundations; built it skyward
  stone by stone.
It is ours, not to slave in, but to master and to own.
While the union makes us strong.

In our hands is placed a power greater than their
  hoarded gold,
Greater than the might of armies, magnified a
  thousand-fold.
We can bring to birth a new world from the ashes of
  the old
For the union makes us strong.

56

Workers' representatives, faith leaders, artists and public intellectuals set out visions of a country in which all had work and which worked for all. Dr King put forward a picture of society as 'a widely separated family who have inherited a world house in which we can never live apart' and as 'an inescapable network of mutuality, tied in a single garment of destiny' in which 'injustice anywhere is a threat to justice everywhere'. The narrative of interconnectedness which was actively developed in the long mid-twentieth century provided a paradigm which facilitated the policies of redistribution.

Marshall Ganz, who worked as an organizer with the Student Nonviolent Coordinating Committee and with Cesar Chavez in the National Farm Workers Association, shared with me the process of how the movements of the time secured change. He emphasized three key drivers. The first was that the process had involved challenging power and challenging social norms, and wasn't a non-conflictual process:

> It wasn't kumbaya. Our work against inequality, in civil rights, in workers' rights, was polarizing; polarizing is not only *not bad*, it's essential. The message wasn't just 'we all need to get along'. Unless 'we all need to get along' is grounded in equal worth and power, it's not getting along, it's maintaining dominance. We *upset* people. We were seen as radical. Democracy is rooted in dissent and contention. That positive polarization was the *beginning* of change, of bringing about a more embracive society through it.

The second was that it had required a long-term sustained process of organizing:

> Pop-ups weren't enough – they had to be structured

into organized power. We had to be patient. The Montgomery Bus Boycott took more than a year of people walking to work. The Farm Workers movement took five years before our first victory. We didn't sit around and wait for the big win. In this time we were building our commitment to each other – these processes were the micro-changes needed for macro change. We made loads of mistakes too – organizing is something learnt by doing it, getting it wrong, falling off, getting back on. Learning from mistakes strengthened us. And when we won changes, our victory was not only that we had achieved the win but that we had created greater collective capability. People said, 'We are stronger than we were.' The organizing was much bigger than picket signs or moments of victory, it was about making democracy work in the sense of every person having equal value and equal voice.

The third was that the new story they built was rooted in a combination of anger, hope and justice:

Anger was essential. But grievance wasn't enough alone if people felt they couldn't win. They also had to see hope – not hokey hope but real hope, based on real possibility. We had that combination of being angry at how it was and knowing that together we could change it. And we had a story of us, a moral conviction that our cause was just. That combination is how we bonded with each other, committed to each other, built our power.

People power was fundamental too to the emergence of the welfare state in Europe. The Scandinavian welfare state, for example, is sometimes portrayed as stemming from an essential Nordic character that is seen as innately egalitarian and gentle. In such a portrayal, they are equal because of their cultural character, with no lessons for the unfortunate rest of us who don't like Abba. But such a portrayal is false.

Up until the early twentieth century, there was grinding poverty and great exploitation in Scandinavia. (Many Americans are descended from Scandinavians who fled starvation!) By strengthening their power through rural collectives and through unions, Scandinavia's small farmers and workers were able to challenge the power of elites. The elites did not accept this challenge at first. Instead, they organized for troops to come out to stop workers' protests and strikes. Norway's government even organized a militia of strike breakers. Strikers were killed, but in the end people's organizing triumphed. What created the conditions for the compromise and concession and for the egalitarianism we see as so Scandinavian today was massive pressure from below. *Not* blonde hair! The Scandinavian story can be a powerful lesson for anyone who dreams of a fairer society.

Britain had downward trajectory on inequality from 1867 right up until the 1970s, as Branko Milanović points out in his powerful book *Global Inequality*. The Second World War generated a profound moment to boost and bolster this transformation, but the progress made in the decades before and the decades after illustrate that we cannot ascribe, as is sometimes implied, the war as the only cause. Inequality was tackled as a result of organizing from the ground up. Churches, cooperatives and unions were key. Unions secured better pay and conditions: as Winston Churchill noted in 1909, 'where you have no organization, no parity of bargaining, the good employer is undercut by the bad, and the bad by the worst — this is not progress, but progressive degeneration.' Union organizing was key to making politically possible the transformation of the economy and society, both in birthing a new party and in pressuring all parties from below.

Tackling inequality in Britain was supported as well by a powerful new story in which insecurity would be removed and a life of dignity secured for all, and common institutions would provide education, health and transport to people of all classes. This story wasn't just told in books and pamphlets but on posters and in pictures and music. Trade unionists organized brass bands, wrote songs, and embroidered banners to set out their vision for a more equal society. In the early twentieth century, suffragette Sylvia Pankhurst's watercolours of women cotton mill and pottery workers highlighted their struggle for dignified working conditions. In the 1940s, the Archbishop of Canterbury, William Temple, coined the phrase 'welfare state'. The profound reshaping of society required far more than a policy debate; it required the displacement in the collective imagination of one story by another. Importantly, the narrative for the new society was not only a modernist one – it involved restoring something deeper, building a post-individualist future rooted in the values of a real or imagined pre-individualist past.

Following independence, and intimately entwined with that independence, African and Asian countries also took bold action to tackle inequality. While it is often the names of great national leaders that dominate how major steps to tackle inequality are remembered, organizing from below was key to their realization. In Ghana, organizing by cocoa workers not only led to the cocoa board protecting their incomes, but also led to the rollout of free education, first to cocoa workers and later to everyone. As the World Social Science Report notes, sometimes the process leading to reductions in inequality was very visibly conflictual – in Malaysia, for example, 'the highspeed redistribution in the 1970s and 1980s was born out of widespread rioting in 1969, as the country's ethnic Malay majority protested about its economic and social marginalization' – while at other times it was more collaborative – in Mauritius, for example, 'the government developed "OECD-style social protection", working with a large and active trade union movement to introduce centralized wage bargaining, price controls on socially sensitive items, and generous social security, especially for the elderly.'

While the route differed, in each case the existence of powerful pressure below was essential. Interestingly, it has been found by experts like Leonard Wantchekon of Princeton and Erica Chenoweth of Harvard that non-violent movements had an important advantage over violent movements in fostering more equal societies afterwards, because violent movements led to a concentration of power, and so to an emphasis on hierarchy and a vertical politics, whereas non-violent movements required a building of a distributed leadership and mass participation that could support a more democratic way of politics. In other words, when change was brought about by mass power, its consequences were more democratic, inclusive, accountable and redistributive. Inequality was fought more successfully by mass movements than by vanguards.

Progress in tackling inequality in African and Asian countries after independence was also rooted in a narrative of the meaning of independence and of national destiny. Anti-colonial movements' visions had not just been about replacing foreign leaders with local ones. Their dreams had been to replace landgrabbing by the rich with fair land redistribution to the poor, cramped slums with room to move, painful hunger with full stomachs, squalor with dignity, exploitation with decent work, corporate impunity with workers' rights, inequality with equality, hopelessness with hope, and shame with self-worth. After all, unions and progressive social movements had often played an essential role in the movement for independence – the Ghana TUC, for example, had been a driving force. There were many disappointments in living up to this ideal, but in countries like Zambia, Tanzania and Sri Lanka, amongst others, attempts to tackle inequality achieved real progress. Political independence was not seen as the end but as the first stage: achieving greater equality was core to honouring those who had made a sacrifice for freedom, and core to fulfilling the national destiny. Citizens in newly independent countries were clear that the role of the new governments was to reshape society by tackling inequality. When later the era of adjustment came, tackling inequality was excised from many countries' mainstream narratives of nationhood, where once it had been inseparable.

The progress made across so many different countries and contexts in tackling inequality during the Golden Age demonstrates that there is nowhere where beating inequality is impossible. There was much that could have been done better, of course. One strategic flaw was that some of the public institutions of the Golden Age which successfully brought societies from grotesque inequalities into basic human decency by providing utilities, services and infrastructure, did then become somewhat calcified, and, as people's expectations went up (especially as new generations grew up without direct personal memory of the time before those institutions), the institutions did not manage to keep up with people's demands of them. When those institutions did not respond well to popular calls to be more accountable, flexible and human-centred, this made those institutions and their defenders vulnerable to the allegation that *they* were the new form of top-down stifling power. This shortcoming, in turn, was very effectively taken advantage of by a new group whose real aim was not to democratize the institutions, but to roll them back.

The progress of the Golden Age was brought to an end, as we'll now examine. But as we recount how we were beaten, we won't just rage at our opponents; we will see what they can teach us.

When the forces for inequality inflicted our biggest defeat, and what we can learn from our opponents

From the 1980s, across much of the world, progress that had been made tackling inequality began to be undone. As the UN's World Social Science Report noted, 'the recent increase in economic inequalities seems to find its origin in the 1980s and 1990s, when the neoliberal paradigm became dominant in Western countries. It later spread gradually to other parts of the world, in the context of the globalization and financialization of the economy.' This was not because technology changed everything, nor because of impersonal historical forces, nor was it an accident. It was the deliberate pursuit of an agenda – neoliberalism – and it had planners, communicators and funders. Talking about this period can make those of us working to tackle inequality wallow in our loss. But we need instead to ask what we can learn from the methods that helped neoliberalism win.

It is rightly recorded that the neoliberals benefitted from crises – first the oil crisis of the 1970s, and then the debt crisis of the 1980s. But what they really benefitted from was their *readiness* for those crises. They had lots of money of course – but that will *always* be an unfair advantage held by those whose agenda facilitates the concentration of wealth. So, apart from having luck and money, what else did they get right? They developed an audacious plan, a strong network to pursue it, and a resonant new myth to secure its acceptance.

The neoliberals were bold. Initially they were treated as cranks, but their experience of facing derision and hostility did not lead them to temper their ambition. They were not interested in limiting their calls for change to those which at the time were considered realistic. They did not seek only to challenge gingerly minor aspects of the Golden Age consensus, they took on the whole agenda. Outriders got ahead of the curve and said things that sounded impossible at first, but over time (and with, of course, a lot of resourcing) they shifted the public conversation, and later they became the authors of a new norm. As we look back, their dauntlessness can be seen to have been vindicated as a strategy.

They understood the power of collective action; thus, they sought to strengthen it among themselves and constrain it for others. They set up networks like the

Mont Pelerin Society because, even as avowed individualists, they knew that they could not win as isolated individuals and would need to cooperate with each other to achieve their shared goal.

They put great efforts into undermining unionization, because without unions each individual worker has only their own personal weak negotiating power. As Economic Policy Institute President Thea Lee explained when we met, 'a lot of the changes put in place in the neoliberal shift undermined the ability of working people to bargain effectively with their employers for their fair share of the wealth that they create'. Countries which more effectively resisted this, which held out more against that trend of deunionization, also held out more against rising inequality.

Neoliberals worked to limit people's participation and organization because, as their guru Friedman once acknowledged frankly, 'a democratic society, once established, destroys a free economy'. That is, ensuring the neoliberal version of *freedom in the marketplace* required undermining people's *freedom to associate*; ensuring untrammelled commerce would necessitate a little trammelling of human beings.

But the neoliberals did not triumph only through suppression, and *could not* have. They needed millions of people to accept and even welcome what was a shift of power against their own interests. For this, neoliberals developed a powerful new story. That story went well beyond economic policy because they realized that what was really at stake was a clash of values. As Hayek and his colleagues had noted in their Statement of Aims for the Mont Pelerin Society back in 1947, the underpinnings of economics were not 'confined to economic doctrines' but were 'part of a movement of ideas which find expression in the field of morals, philosophy and the interpretation of history' and that therefore they 'must direct their attention to these wider ideas as well' and mould a new 'widely accepted moral code'.

As modern myth-makers they were hugely successful. They developed a high-level intellectual agenda, but that alone did not bring them a breakthrough. So they developed a way to sell their rather cold economic approach as being rooted in a much warmer yearning for freedom and respectability, connecting individualism with nationalism and tradition. They did so through stories told in the mass media from magazines to movies. It is no coincidence that the most famous voice of neoliberalism was not one of its intellectuals like Milton Friedman, but an actor, Ronald Reagan.

They talked the language of iconoclasm and liberty. They talked of 'rebelling' against the power of doctors or teachers or government officials (but, of course, not of rebelling against the power of the big money). The word 'meritocracy', which had originally been used satirically, was turned into a hugely successful fabrication that if the state let corporations do as they wished, then anyone could rise to the top through effort and talent. This meant that anyone *not* at the top had only themselves to blame, and anyone who sat at the top 'deserved' all they had because they had 'made it there' by themselves. The fact that social mobility actually decreases with high inequality mattered less than the power of the fiction told in films, taught in schools, and repeated on the news. The policies flowed from, and depended on, the myths. The neoliberal project's success was rooted in its rewiring how we talked about society.

Their victory was breath-taking. Compare the 1950s – where in the US, France and the UK, for example, both main parties accepted the consensus that the state must serve to counter big disparities of wealth – to the 1990s, where in all three countries both main parties accepted the new consensus that it must not. Indeed, neoliberalism so upended the terms of 'left' and 'right' that the economic approaches of the so-called left party governments of the 1990s were in many respects to the 'right' of the so-called right party governments of the 1950s! That was a true mark of triumph. Indeed, these two periods – the Golden Age and the neoliberal era – mark how two different sides succeeded in turn in what Gramsci called 'hegemonizing the discourse', that is, dominating the popular story that is told and determining the bounds of mainstream debate.

Reflecting on when and how we *won* in the fight against inequality is vital to helping us win again; but, so too, is reflecting on when and how we got *beaten*. Don't get mad, get *even*.

Learning from history in the fight against inequality

The experiences of our ancestors illustrate shared lessons about the kinds of approaches that can successfully fight inequality. Every place and every struggle were unique and different, of course, but, as Edward Said wrote, 'the task for the critical scholar is not to separate one struggle from another, but to connect them.'

Crises were often important – creating critical junctures or moments of possibility – but crises alone were never enough to secure success for those fighting inequality. The 1929 crisis was followed by progressive change in the US, but was followed by fascism in central Europe. The oil and debt crises helped facilitate neoliberalism. Movements needed to build *before the crisis came* in order to be ready to seize the moment to beat back inequality.

All successful movements against inequality faced hostility from the powerful, and therefore depended on people's willingness to get into trouble. John Lewis, who helped lead the US civil rights movement, describes how, as a child, he was urged by his mother 'don't get in the way, don't get in trouble', but that, as a teenager, inspired by activists fighting inequality, he realized that making change required him to 'get in trouble, good trouble, necessary trouble.' So too, the landless workers who demanded access to land in Latin America, and the Suffragettes who struggled for votes for women in Britain, were all treated as 'troublemakers' before they were recognized for prompting needed change. Governments did not act with the determination needed to tackle inequality without a push from the rest of us, and consistently resisted that push at first. Marjorie Stoneman Douglas, who worked with movements for women's rights, civil rights, migrant rights and the environment across the twentieth century, summed up her key lesson as 'be a nuisance where it counts'. When power was challenged, the backlash was often fierce – but as history demonstrates, that backlash could be an indicator of progress.

Victories against inequality were rooted too in mass

organizing – the change in each case was collective, never individual – because winning the battle against inequality has required power, which for ordinary people is only ever collective. Progress against inequality often involved compromise and negotiations – but what has been crucial for those fighting inequality was having the strength required in those compromises and negotiations. Likewise, 'concessions' by the powerful were *not* the same as generosity; the *need* for concessions stemmed from the fact that elite power was weakened because people had organized. Having allies on the inside often helped those working for greater equality, but that was never enough – as a *group*, the dominant had to be pushed. As the father of history, the Ancient Greek writer Thucydides put it, 'the quality of justice depends on the equality of power to compel', as when power is unchecked, 'the strong do what they can and the weak suffer what they must.'

Fear of an *external* threat was an important factor in several cases, of course – the Cold War fear of communism helped encourage Western countries to be more egalitarian, for example – but in these cases, too, progress *also* depended on there being organized people *within* those countries whose potential challenge was feared enough by elites to force them to make concessions.

The stories that people developed, the pictures they painted of a more equal world, were a crucial enabler and shaper of change too. The language of shared values and shared experience served to illustrate our common humanity. Trade unionists, suffragettes, anti-colonialists, activists and religious communities created songs, poems, posters, badges and banners setting out a vision in which the extremes of privilege and exclusion would be replaced by a society that worked for all. Then, in the 1970s and 1980s, neoliberals successfully changed the conversation from community to individualism.

Looking back, we can observe how victories against inequality did not just 'happen', and were not just 'given', but were *won*, by ordinary people who were challenging, organized, and painted a picture of the world that could be.

History demonstrates that the fight against inequality is winnable, but also that no victory is final. As one civil rights song reminded people:

> Freedom doesn't come like a bird on the wing
> It doesn't come down like the summer rain,
> Freedom, freedom is a hard-won thing.
> You've got to work for it, fight for it,
> Day and night for it,
> And every generation has to win it again.

Now, too, we must make our own history.

Journal: Great campaigns have lots of things in common, but they're not the things we're often taught

When I was young, I got involved in campaigns because I was passionate about them. But when I became an NGO professional, I was taught to be much more focused on realism, cool-headed analysis, and the careful assessment of strategies. What matters, I was told, is what works.

70

So, in that spirit, I talked to four leaders whose campaigns have definitely succeeded in order to find out what it was that really made the difference. Jay Naidoo led the South African trade union movement's struggle against apartheid; Ann Pettifor headed the Jubilee 2000 campaign to cancel third world debt; Lilian Njehu worked alongside the Nobel Prize-winning environmentalist Wangari Maathai in the campaign to save Kenya's forests; Kumuti Majhi is a tribal leader from Niyamgiri in India who defeated the Vedanta corporation's plans to mine his people's land.

As each of these campaigners were at pains to point out, all successes are partial and impermanent, and no victory is won by one person alone, but nevertheless these are winners. They are all different, but they do have lots of things in common. It's just that they're not the things that I'd been taught.

First of all, I asked them if they knew that they would win when they began their campaigns. I thought they might set out the practical reasons behind their confidence, the power mapping they had done and the assessments they had made. But none of them described anything like that at all. Pettifor told me 'No, I was sure at the beginning that we *could not* win', and shared how there had been an internal argument over the branding of the campaign as Jubilee 2000 because she and others 'could not see how we could make debt a big issue with that identity in just five years ... but

I was wrong. Our identity, and its deep symbolism embedded in Islam, Judaism and Christianity, was vital to our success.'

Others said that they *did* know they would win, but not because they'd conducted any formal planning or analysis. Instead, it was a matter of heartfelt conviction. 'This was the land that our forefathers died for', as Njehu put it. 'Because we have faith in our people and "Niyam Raja"' was Majhi's response, 'We worship Niyamgiri as our living God and under no circumstances will we leave our God. Our struggle has gone through many ups and downs, but we never stopped – even during the worst time of our life.' Naidoo described how he got involved in the struggle against apartheid because of Steve Biko. 'Steve didn't give us a project plan or a log frame or a budget', he told me, 'he gave us a direction to follow, and pride. He taught us to love ourselves, and that we had nothing to lose but our chains.'

That's a clue to the second lesson of their experience: all successful campaigns move backwards as well as forwards, and when times were tough these leaders drew strength not from a plan but from a deeper moral force. Majhi shared that what drove his community was the 'determination to protect our "motherland" for generations to come.' Pettifor said something similar: 'as someone born and raised in Africa, I was deeply invested in the campaign, believing it to be one of moral, economic and social injustice.

That conviction drove me on. Although I am not religious, I had deep faith that with commitment, and in community with others, righteousness and justice would prevail.' Njehu described how her group's 'faith meant we could not fear death.' These are phrases that are hardly ever used in standard training for campaigners or reports about what works.

Thirdly, what brought victory was not individual smarts but collective strength. As Naidoo explained, the power of mass mobilization and popular organization is also vital. 'To bring change, we organized, factory by factory, street by street', he said, to 'build around people's priorities and to find their priorities by asking.' Njehu emphasized how success was rooted in being 'a grassroots movement, built up from ordinary women fighting for their families, saving the wood they need for cooking for their children, saving the land on which they depended. It was their felt need.' People power was central to all these victories, and central to people power was unity.

Majhi described a village meeting where company officials 'tried to purchase our people by providing meat and liquor, but not a single person spoke in favour of the company.' Likewise, a protest planned by Pettifor and her colleagues outside the G8 meeting in Birmingham in 1998 looked like it might not attract many people after the UK government tried to put them off with the message that 'the G8 leaders would instead spend that day in a castle miles away. But suddenly, as I stood outside Birmingham Station, I saw thousands of supporters pour out. The government tactic had failed, and the Prime Minister was obliged to return to Birmingham to meet with the representatives of the 100,000 Jubilee 2000 supporters.' Lobbying, however smart, is only ever effective when matched by direct action by substantial groups of determined people who stand together, shoulder to shoulder.

Fourth, all refused to have the campaigns' agendas shaped by donors even when this meant that they had to work with very meagre resources. As Njehu put it, 'when donors came to us to change our plans, we said we won't take your money because we don't want to follow your plan.' 'Money is important', she added, 'but it can't change your idea. You can campaign without money if people understand it as their campaign. If they don't see it as their problem, you can't give them money to understand it as their felt need.' Naidoo warned that an increasing focus on donors is already weakening many social justice organizations: 'Now is the moment of truth for social movements, trade unions, progressive forces and NGOs. They have to break with the conservatism and bureaucracies that have made them bystanders in this grand clash between overwhelming majority and a tiny, insulated class of super-rich', he said.

Fifth, I asked each leader what advice they would give to their younger selves. None of them mentioned the advantages of more formal training. Instead, they spoke of the determination required to stay engaged for the inevitable long haul of campaigning. 'Never give up', Majhi said, 'whatever may be the circumstances, however much they may oppress you. Just continue your journey and keep the community interest on the top of your individual interest. Any struggle to be successful needs sacrifice and there is no short route to that.' Pettifor's advice to her younger self was particularly touching: 'Your single-minded determination was laudable', she said, 'but you would have got further if you had acquired some diplomatic skills.'

Lastly, all of them emphasized that their stories are full of failures and screw-ups – and that makes their successes seem less impossible to learn from. My favourite comes from Naidoo: 'On the day Nelson Mandela was released', he confessed to me in a bar in Tunis, 'I was supposed to look after him. But it wasn't planned, it all happened so fast, there was so much going on, and I lost him.' 'You lost him?' I asked. 'Yeah, we didn't have phones then so we couldn't get hold of him. I had no idea where he was.' 'You lost Mandela?' 'Yeah.' 'You led the trade union struggle, you helped topple apartheid, but you lost Mandela.' 'Yeah, I know.'

Overall, if campaigning for justice is a social science, then these lessons suggest that it's 'less science' and 'more social.' Each of the successful campaigners' stories revealed that they had tapped into something deeper, something more profound, and worked to harness it for change because, as Angela Davis once put it, 'I am *no longer* accepting the things I cannot change. I am changing the things I cannot accept.' Through their wisdom they have helped me to rediscover the spirit I had been taught to let go.

How we'll win the fight against inequality again

'It always seems impossible until it is done'
The policies to fight inequality, and how to secure them
Overcome deference
Build power together
Create a new story

'It always seems impossible until it is done'

Another quiz: Who did a 1966 Gallup Opinion poll show was viewed *unfavourably* by 63 per cent of Americans?

It was Martin Luther King.

I highlight this for two reasons. The first is that, because by 2011 Dr King was viewed unfavourably by only 4 per cent of Americans, people often read the recent consensus back into history and assume that he was always mainstream, and learn therefore a completely false lesson, that change comes from people and movements who never offend anyone; whereas the true lesson of Dr King and of other changemakers is that fighting inequality requires us to disrupt, to confront power and to take on prevailing norms. The second reason I highlight that poll is that it helps to remind us, at a time when our struggle against inequality might seem impossible, of the many times when previous movements for social progress were seen as impossible, before they started to be written about in retrospect as if they had been inevitable.

The obscene inequality we see today is sometimes seen as inevitable and unchangeable – because of human nature, or because of technological changes, or because the vicious cycle can never be beaten. One of those who has come to be associated with the 'it's inevitable' view of ever-rising inequality is the great French economist Thomas Piketty, whose brilliant book *Capital* set out in stark detail the current economic trajectory and how inequality begets further inequality. So, when he visited London for a lecture, I asked him if changes in inequality are essentially out of our control, or are from choices, and therefore whether anything can be done. Given his reputation as a pessimist, his answer was surprising to the audience, and hopeful. 'It's not random', he replied, 'it's about politics. The resurgence of inequality after 1980 is due largely to *political* shifts, especially in regard to taxation and finance. My conclusion therefore is *not* pessimistic. Democratic processes can fix inequality. It's not easy but it's possible.' Piketty's focus on democratic processes is quite right. And by democratic processes he does not just mean elections; he means active citizens' organizing – as did Dr King.

We are faced with a structural challenge of dominance by powerful elites who will not make way unless they are pressured to, but with the right pressure they will shift. Inequality can be beaten, because *we* can beat it, together. It might seem impossible now but, as Nelson Mandela noted, 'it always seems impossible until it is done.'

The policies to fight inequality, and how to secure them

Government action is essential to win the fight against inequality. When we say that winning the fight depends on you, we do *not* mean that you can win it as an individual through your own personal lifestyle choices. And when we say that it depends on how you work *with others*, we do not mean that a group of true believers can take on the challenge of inequality by dropping out of society and establishing a self-sufficient isolated idyll. The struggle against inequality is not about *whether* we relate to each other, it is about *how* we relate to each other. It is about *structure*, and to shift structure – to shift relations at work, access to services and the distribution of wealth – we need to drive action by the state.

The siren song, sung in the name of empowerment, that communities can 'fix their problems by themselves' if they 'keep the government out', is disconnected from reality, hugely regressive, and unjust. If ordinary people are 'left alone' by government, the services and infrastructure they develop for themselves will always be under-resourced; and if the rich are 'left alone' by government, their vast accumulation will be left untouched – which is, frankly, why they fund those who call for it. Government needs to be put right, not pushed back. Beating back inequality can't be done without it. We need active, strong, *accountable* governments.

How we'll win the fight against inequality again

'There are many instruments that governments have to address inequality', UNDP Latin America and Caribbean Director Luis Felipe López-Calva explained to me, 'they need look at *before* the market, *in* the market and *after* the market. Where people are going to the labour market, they have to be equipped in terms of education, health and other aspects. But then the markets need to be regulated so that they do not exclude and that they lead to socially desirable outcomes. But even after that there are other instruments that governments have at hand and should use to redistribute ex-post.'

So the strategy for tacking inequality is a strategy rooted in securing a broad set of inequality-busting policies. Tackling inequality starts with *national* policy because domestic questions of distribution increasingly determine whether, as countries become better off, their people do too. At the same time, the global impact of climate change, of the large multinationals who control more wealth than many countries, and of the world's tax havens, necessitates that policies also connect *internationally*.

The policy mix is broad but it is not a mystery. Of course, policies must be tailored to context, and are best generated country by country, not mandated from above. There are, however, several common lessons. History, grassroots demand and policy analysis all point in a similar direction, one that we illustrate below.

We can see from precedents the need to build from, and go further than, the kinds of policies introduced in the 2000s in Brazil which increased jobs and salaries for the poor, increased social protection, expanded education, redistributed income and land, and tackled discrimination; and the precedents across the world in the long mid-twentieth international 'Golden Age', including expansion of public services, progressive taxation, facilitating unionization, and limiting the excessive concentration of wealth in a small number of hands. From grassroots civil society organizations, we hear a complementary set of demands repeatedly made: free health and education for all; jobs with dignity; land; cutting VAT and exempting necessities; making the rich and corporations pay their fair share of tax; and compensation for loss and damage for communities hit by climate change. Such demands need of course to be fleshed out to be workable policy – and this is what policy analysts in NGOs and academia have done.

A report I oversaw when at ActionAid, *The Price of Privilege: Extreme Wealth, Unaccountable Power, and the Fight for Equality*, laid out some of the policies needed to reduce inequality. These included: increasing investment in public services including health, education and early child care and in public infrastructure; providing social protection including child benefit and old age pensions; widening access to land and redistributing large private land holdings; shifting away from indirect taxes, making income taxes more progressive, and closing tax loopholes and tax holidays; raising minimum wages to living wages; and recognizing, redistributing and reducing women's unpaid care burden. Given the extent of the inequality crisis we are in and the need to shift *power* away from the one per cent and towards the rest of the population, the report also proposed: strengthening trade union rights; instituting a wealth tax; increasing corporate democracy by increasing employees' decision-making role in companies; instituting a maximum wage

81

proportional to the wage paid to companies' most junior workers; and limiting private finance for political parties and political campaigns.

The excellent Commitment to Reduce Inequality Index by Development Finance International and Oxfam showcases examples of government actions to address inequality: South Korea's increase in taxes on the wealthy, expansion of pro-poor public spending and increase in the minimum wage; Ethiopia's education investment; Indonesia's increase in the minimum wage and spending on health. The Index also highlights government policies that are most exacerbating inequality – how the freezing of social spending by the new Brazilian government is undermining the progress made by its predecessor; how the US government's slashing of corporation tax is one of the biggest giveaways to the one per cent in history.

Beyond these headlines, the Commitment to Reduce Inequality Index details, for 157 countries based on 27 indicators, how their social, fiscal and labour policies measure up and what more they each need to do to fulfil the international promise to tackle inequality. There's even an interactive map at inequalityindex.org.

The climate movement has powerfully described how unchecked climate change will further widen inequality, and have explained how the policies needed to tackle climate change are ones which help fight inequality. These include taking on the consumption of the richest people who, as Stefan Gössling of Lund University has calculated, produce 10,000 times more carbon emissions than the average person. And they include also a massive investment in public transport and public infrastructure which will reduce inequality in at least four ways: generating millions of quality jobs; creating top-quality no-fee common assets and services funded by progressive taxation; improving public health; and even, at a deeper cultural level, fostering the collective experience that comes when people use services together. The tired old debate about 'people vs environment' is over, and the 'just transition' call that unites unions and environmentalists has been detailed, costed and modelled – ready for whenever the policy-makers are.

In addition to some great books and papers by NGOs and academics, there are also some excellent policy reports by the United Nations: radical proposals are no longer buried deep inside to avoid censors; even the titles speak of 'Financing a Global Green New Deal' and 'Options to Expand Social Investments in 187 Countries'.

The conversation on policies to tackle inequality is the most exciting it has been in a generation. And there is a key role for producing evidence and policy recommendations to shift the sense of the possible, support allies within governments, and support progressive advocacy. But just as we must reject the fantasy that we can beat inequality without action by government, so too we must reject the fantasy that government will act if only it receives the right policy recommendations backed by the right evidence. That is not how transformative policy-making works. We need to go beyond developing the list of what we would *like* government leaders to do, and work out how we will *get* them to do it. To date, most of the work looking at redressing inequality has been policy-focused, not politics-focused; but we are, to be frank, not suffering from a dearth of ideas about what a government committed to tackling inequality could do. The key challenge now is how to make such change *possible*.

It is true that nothing changes without a politician standing for it, but that does not mean relying on politicians. Policy-making is not working for ordinary people because it has been captured by elites, and we need to claim it back. Oxfam International Executive Director Winnie Byanyima put it to me like this: 'Change will come from people organizing, because inequality is about power, it's political, and it's only going to be resolved by people challenging the power that has been captured by a few.'

Unless ordinary people build their power to hold governments to account, transformational policy change will not be pursued, and any positive policies which are enacted will be inadequately followed through and be too easily reversible. Jay Naidoo, who founded the trade union coalition which helped bring down apartheid, reminded a group of young campaigners against inequality how change like this is won: 'It's not about how brilliant your argument is – no one cedes power because of a great PowerPoint. What matters is the balance of power between your side, the people's side, in the confrontation and negotiations with the other side, the side of the elite. The truly effective civil society organizations will be those that work out how to organize people in the twenty-first century.' Social and popular will precedes political will.

The approach to how we advance change needs to be commensurate with the scale of transformation required. The scale of change entailed can only come about through pressure from below – it is the only way it ever has. It's clear that a strategy that sought *any* progressive change through evidence sharing and insider advocacy alone, blind to issues of interests and power, would be deeply flawed. From officials of Thailand's Ministry of Health, for example, I heard how it was organizing by groups of patients, especially people living with HIV/AIDS, which generated the political momentum that led to access to affordable medicine – in the face of great opposition from pharmaceutical companies and Western governments – and then to the introduction of universal health care – which the World Bank had told the government it could not afford to do. Similarly, free education in Kenya, the defeat of the Free Trade Area of the Americas, and the international decision to 'Drop the Debt' all came from the build-up of collective power to challenge elite power.

Even more so, a strategy that sought to overcome *inequality* without building up people's power to press for it would be completely disconnected from history and logic. Inequality is not just one progressive cause among many. It is the structure, the meta-problem, that holds back every progressive change. Reversing rising inequality is not just about changing the rules but about changing who gets to make the rules. It is not a polite theoretical debate or standard-issue lobby demand. It is the imbalance of power, and it can only be tackled by building a countervailing power. As President Obama said in a speech to the UN, 'the wealthy like to keep things as they are, and have disproportionate influence.'

Kenyan activist Njoki Njehu, who started in grass-roots mobilization with activist Wangari Maathai defending people's forest land and human rights, and then went on to lead organizations in DC, shared with a group of us why she left DC and went back to organizing at the grassroots. 'DC can be a great place to fight for change, but you can also get lost in circles. You can have a campaign with great reports and media but will change no lives, until you start to organize people. Don't get lost in influence peddling. Power for change always comes from below.'

It is sometimes said that the one thing about tackling inequality is that there is *not* one thing. That is, no individual policy victory is enough to win the fight against inequality, and so the process of organizing needs to be an ongoing one. The most effective groups I have witnessed and walked alongside in the fight against inequality have all developed a variation of this two-fold strategy: first, to organize to win the particular struggle they're fighting at a specific moment, perhaps a higher minimum wage or land reform; but secondly, and most importantly, through winning that specific struggle, to strengthen their capability for the next one, and the next one. Through this, they effectively navigate influencing a series of institutions and enabling a series of policies, while cyclically improving their own proficiency in doing so, building the support base on which their power rests, and building confidence that change is possible. Of course, the specific wins do matter – both in the immediate difference they make and because without seeing some successes it is hard to maintain morale. But each win is only one part of a larger strategy. That's what makes movements different from single-issue campaigns.

To successfully advance a series of radically different policies, we need also to help paint a picture of how we can live together more fairly. We need the specific demands, but we also need the larger vision that sets out what a good society can be. As Danny Sriskandarajah shared, 'We need to lift our gaze from the skirmishes to the bigger picture – we are at a moment of a peculiar, globalized, stratified economy and particularly vulgar forms of accumulation and greed. We need to build alternative stories.'

The instruments for rectifying inequality are policies, the mechanism is government, but the only force able to ensure government delivers is *us*. How? Three essential elements stand out that we will now look at in turn: overcome deference, build power together, and create a new story.

Overcome deference

Though victories against inequality end up with some kind of new consensus, they depend on breaking an old one, in defiance of authority. So the first thing we need to do to fight inequality is to overcome deference.

Revd Liz Theoharis is a biblical scholar and pastor, who beams with goodness. She is a co-founder of the Poor People's Campaign, the largest social justice movement in the US today. After a public event I had organized with her, I sat down with her to understand more about her personal story. She recalled to me how she had been instructed to lay off activism by her seniors right from her time in seminary, where her supervisors even warned her that she would never be made a church minister. She shared how even now the Poor People's Campaign continues to be pressed not to stir things up too much by authority figures from the churches, from the political parties and from state institutions; and how she calmly reminds them that, in the fight against inequality, insubordination is essential – and a moral obligation. As she departed to head off to a series of mass meetings across the other side of the country, I asked if she might be able to join a forthcoming international gathering of activists in Zambia. 'I'd love to, but I don't know when I'll get my passport back', she replied, 'it was taken from me the last time I got arrested.' The taxi driver looked horrified and frightened. 'It's OK, it was for a good cause', I tried to reassure him, 'she's a church minister, she was doing God's work.' He didn't look at all convinced, and Liz didn't even try to explain herself. She just smiled.

Overcoming deference is so challenging because it has been inculcated in us, in families, schools, places of work, and in many of our institutions. It reflects our assumptions that the powerful know best, and that their power is representative of a natural authority. We want to be close to power, to be respectable, so we adopt isomorphic mimicry: we try to look like who we are trying to impress. The undeferential, meanwhile, are labelled 'uppity', rude or anti-social. 'Society has been bent to the idea that one group of people deserves to be treated better than the rest of us', Zambian musician and activist Pilato shared, 'and so it is not only the perpetrators who defend the status quo – many ordinary people do too, and those who go against the social norms are treated as outlaws.'

Much greater outrage is expressed about the disruptiveness of those challenging injustices than about the injustices themselves. South African activist Meshack Mbangula has had to learn not to be put off by being regularly (and unlawfully) intercepted by police and told he must turn around when travelling to support communities challenging mining corporations. Environmental activists are told that it is their disruption that prevents a reasoned debate. Trade unionists are told that it is their strike that is preventing improvements to conditions at work. Sometimes the discouragement of activists is framed as being only about 'the way' that they are pointing out the injustice: powerful people issue 'friendly advice' to tell the disruptors to quieten down because they are 'only harming the cause', which they claim will be achieved through patience and quietude. The powerful never tire of telling civil society to be more civil. But there is *no way* that ends the criticism of 'the way': as Dr King noted, 'frankly I have yet to engage in a direct action movement that was "well-timed" in the view of those who have not suffered unduly; this "wait!" has almost always meant "never".' We need to be ready to be 'difficult'.

One way that can help us overcome deference is to remind ourselves that today's historical heroes of social progress were yesterday's awkward squad. Whenever people ask me 'why can't Black Lives Matter be more like Dr King?' or 'why can't today's women's marchers be more like the Suffragettes?', I remind the questioners that all these icons, who are *today* sanitized as unchallenging, *terrified* the powerful *at the time* because they refused to be deferential. Just look, for example, at all the heroes recently selected to grace US bank notes in celebration of the end of slavery, the achievement of civil rights, and votes for women: Harriet Tubman, Susan B. Anthony, Sojourner Truth, Alice Paul, Martin Luther King. All of them were activist troublemakers who the establishment of the time not only resisted, but tried to crush.

Perhaps one day the establishment will organize stamps and holidays to celebrate the activists who they currently label as militants, just as they currently honour yesteryear's victories that their predecessors fought just as hard to prevent, and lost. (Indeed, one silver lining to the cloud of the current US administration's delay in the issuing of the long overdue Harriet Tubman banknote is that it reminds us that she boldly took on hegemonic power.) As US activist Bree Newsome pointed out: '160 years ago slavery was legal, normalized and embedded in society. Abolitionists were considered radical. 60 years ago, Jim Crow was law, was normalized. Protesters were considered radical.' Bree took that history of radical courage to heart when in 2015, weeks after a white supremacist had murdered nine parishioners at a South Carolina black church, Bree went to the South Carolina Statehouse, climbed thirty feet up the flagpole, and grabbed and took down the Confederate flag herself. She too was described as a troublemaker. But soon after, the state governor signed a bill to take the flag down permanently.

Taking up a more challenging approach involves needing to be willing to have periods in the wilderness, just as all those acknowledged as changemakers today once did. As Danny Sriskandarajah, director of Civicus, the global civil society network, shared: 'If you are not ready or able to take the short-term hit on popularity or access by sticking your neck out, you can't do big change.' And it incurs serious risks. While it may seem so much easier to avoid controversy, Dinah Musindarwezo, director of African feminist network

Femnet, told me, 'an unwillingness to suffer – a lack of courage – is what most holds back movement building.' Zambian musician and activist Pilato puts it this way: 'Yes everyone is scared, and I am too, but what gives me courage is that I have something that I am more scared of. I am scared of going to prison but I am more scared of the country going to prison. People want quiet, but when our quiet enables one group of people to become so powerful to do whatever they want to us, then that quiet has become enabling, and then I know I must be loud, to remind people of the power that we have when we use it.'

This is not about being a Rebel Without a Cause. There is value to work from the inside as well as outside. In my own work, I have been involved with and witnessed the value of NGOs making incremental change by helping governments in fulfilling their responsibilities by sharing evidence and experience with them, and by helping connect those making decisions with those affected by them. When I met a few years back with the government on the island of Zanzibar in Tanzania they told me that the work my colleagues were doing in helping schools to prevent child marriage was a crucial support to the government's strategy. But addressing injustice can't be limited to supporting those with power as their helpful advisors. On that same visit I also met on the Tanzanian mainland with people whose land and homes were threatened a landgrab by a Swedish company. We faced a lot of heat for speaking out in support of the community – and the community faced even greater heat. Even many of the powerful figures who defined themselves as our allies on the inside questioned whether such an approach might be counter-productive. But shortly afterwards, the principal funder of the landgrab pulled out, problems were recognized, the deal was put on hold, the people's issues started to be heard, and community members felt secure enough to start putting up permanent structures to support their farming again as productive citizens.

Likewise, across the world, I've worked with organizations who have challenged corporations who had not paid their fair share of tax and the systems of tax breaks which deny the resources needed for health and education: when we and others first started raising this issue, we were seen as part of an awkward squad, but now international institutions say that it is their top priority and leading companies say they back the call for fair taxation.

However, in recent years, many NGOs have become too cosy with the establishment, too wary of activism and too awed by authority. They have allowed themselves to be boxed into focusing on projects for development 'delivery' – even though their largest scale impact is not in the number of items of assistance that they provide, or the number of trainings they provide, but in how they support people to claim their rights. Likewise, too much NGO advocacy has wanted so much to look 'neutral' or unthreatening that they have held back from profound challenge. The term 'non-governmental organization' should be a reminder of the one thing NGOs are not: the Government. 'Remember', an NGO colleague used to remind colleagues, 'we don't work for *them*.' NGOs must ward off the temptations of 'access' just as Frodo must resist the temptations of the ring. If you work for an NGO and have not once heard that a government or corporation or other powerful figure is angry with you, you should be angry with yourself. As Tax Justice Network's Alex Cobham told me: 'If we are never accused of being unrealistic or attacked for being too bold, we are doing something wrong. If we are never uncomfortable, that should make us uncomfortable. The hard truth is that changemakers will always be feared – and so if you are never ever feared, you are not a changemaker.' It is the grit in the oyster which makes the pearl.

Overcoming deference is key not only for building effective movements to challenge current elites: it is vital *within* movements too. Organizations which seek to redistribute power and support challenge and accountability need to model that. Failing to do this is a common strategic flaw in social justice movements. For example, a key reason why ANC rule has not reduced economic inequality in South Africa is that the various anti-apartheid movements were too deferential to the leaders after they went into government. Civil society and union leaders were brought into government as ministers and officials, and those brought in counselled those left behind that there was no need for pressure from below anymore, that would only disrupt progress, and so now was the time to practise 'discipline' and not to get in the way of their comrades in government. The consequence was that much of civil society held back from challenging power, and so trickle-down power led to trickle-down economics. It has been the much less deferential movements like Fees Must Fall and the Treatment Action Campaign which have been post-apartheid South Africa's most successful. There is always a need for challenge.

We need to drop the whole idea of stars – even the ones on our side. 'We spend way too much time focusing on identifying and building the philosopher king', organizer Christopher Rutledge summed it up pithily to me, 'and way too little time building the structures and institutions of participation and inclusivity. How many times does history have to prove to us that leaders are fallible and that without building participatory institutions of governance the temptations of power within hierarchical systems are just too great and just too easy to abuse.' Even the leaders most committed to fighting inequality need to be challenged – indeed, they should want it, and if they discourage it, it's a warning signal. As an activist friend remarked to me, 'the thing about heroes is that unless they die they tend to disappoint.' Inequality can never be tackled by one giant – it can only be done by people working together – leaderful, and accountable. In other words, don't look up, look *around*.

The Fight for 15 movement has been a wonderful embodiment of overcoming deference. The idea of a $15 minimum wage is now very mainstream in the US – a talking point in political debates, a pledge by several major companies, a law in a range of cities and states, and hugely popular with almost all demographics and with supporters of both major parties. So it is vital to recall the reception it got when it was started. When campaigners first mooted the idea of a $15 minimum wage, their 'sympathetic' allies in the Obama White House all urged them to drop it quickly, and even among the organizations working for workers the plan was seen by many as unrealistic. 'We had no VIP politicians lined up in support. And there was a culture of union obedience to the interests of Democratic elected officials, of not rocking the boat', union organizer

David Rolf recalled to me. 'We were *literally* laughed at. We were the crazies.' Thankfully, the Fight for 15 activists were undeferential enough to persist.

Thankfully, too, the Fight for 15 movement did not demand deference from others, and was comfortable with not knowing fully how plans would evolve, recognizing that the way in which the movement would develop would be non-linear and *not* according to a central plan. And *that* is why it succeeded. The movement had originally started with retail workers and struggled to take off. It got lift-off with strikes by fast food workers in New York. But then it was *reimagined* by another group of organizers in SeaTac, a small town in Washington State, to be not only a strike aimed at companies but as a ballot campaign for a law for a place with an electorate dominated by airport employees. This was not in any of Fight for 15's original plans, but they welcomed this bottom-up innovation, which when it won locally created the powerful precedent of 'this is now how things are for people in one town, and it's how things can be for you too'. This generated a positive cycle of victories by one group of workers inspiring other groups of workers to start their own actions, and a momentum that continues today.

In El Salvador, I sat down with a group of young activists involved in Plataforma Global, an inspiring network which connects social movement organizers to learn from each other. They shared impressive stories of struggles won or under way against powerful interests like metal and water companies. I asked them to describe the most useful thing they had learnt through the network to enable these successes. They replied by describing what they had *unlearnt*: 'We had been taught before to be passive, to accept what we had been told, to be afraid; here we've been teaching ourselves to unlearn all of that.'

Journal: The unquiet – challenging inequality in Pakistan

They were brought up to be quiet. But they insist upon raising their voice. At a gathering in Lahore of women grassroots activists from different parts of rural and small-town Pakistan, they meet to discuss what they have been doing to challenge the worst inequalities and to hold government to account in their communities. To learn from each other, they take it in turns to share their stories.

I am a schoolteacher, and my school didn't have a boundary wall, or a toilet. So, I met with the local government official and said that it needed to be fixed. He said there were no funds. I said that I would find that out using the Right to Information Act. He organized for the wall and the toilet.

When a man murdered young girls, the police did nothing to arrest him. So, I went to see the police to complain. The murderer's family went to visit my brother to put pressure on me to stop pushing. But my brother supported me. I stood firm. Then six days later the police arrested the killer.

I organized for the women in my village to get ID cards – we could not get them because our

---

marriages were not being recognized as Hindus. It can be difficult to be a Hindu, even harder to be low-caste Hindu. We are called untouchable. But I don't care what they say. I am not afraid.

That's right. If the authorities think we are weak and innocent they ignore us. But if they see that we know our rights, that we are strong, then they act.

In my village there is a piece of land on which some very poor families have been farming for many years. But the government wanted to sell the land from under them. We organized a protest and the local media came. The families were weeping. I went inside to meet the official and urged him to stop the land sale. He asked why. I told him he was a public servant and his salary was paid for by these families' taxes. He laughed and said they pay no taxes; they are too poor. I said every time they buy something, they are paying taxes. Even when they buy a match box, they must pay tax on it. He told me that even if he wanted to stop the sale he could not. But I knew the rules and I told him he could postpone the sale and write to the higher-ups recommending that the families be allowed to stay. We went outside together, and he announced to the media that the sale had been postponed. The families still live on that land.

So much is being written about what is *wrong* in Pakistan, from feudal land ownership, to under-investment in health and education, to tax dodging by the rich, to endemic violence against women, to war. But that is not the only story.

'These small-small things we are changing', explains one of the women. They are an unlikely grouping: they speak different languages, have different religions, come from different backgrounds. 'You see this lady', says one of her friends as she holds her hand, 'she is a landlord's daughter, not like the rest of us who are poor, but she is one of us now.' Her friend smiles: 'And we are getting stronger, because we have learnt. And because we have each other.'

The great eighteenth-century British anti-slavery campaigner William Wilberforce was once asked why he kept on fighting for what seemed to so many to be an unwinnable cause. 'We are too young to realize that certain things are impossible', he replied, 'so we will do them anyway.'

Build power together

Though courage is vital in beating inequality, it is not enough. Inequality is a system of dominance that we can only overcome if we have enough strength. So the second thing we need to do to fight inequality is to build power together.

Organizing is how. An interesting paper demonstrated recently that the weaker the trade unions get in a country, the worse inequality will get; I say it's an interesting paper because it was by the IMF! The data is so clear that it can't be denied. But Billy Bragg's song 'Power in the Union' put it better than any research paper: 'who'll defend the workers who cannot organize?' Building power together is work. It's about methodology, not just philosophy: 'after you get the will you need to get the skill', says Kingian community organizer Charles Alphin, 'you need to build a critical mass.'

#MeToo founder Tarana Burke emphasized to me how 'a movement is not a hashtag, it's not just people saying things; it takes time, organizing, nurturing, being deliberate, feet to the street and being rooted in community.' Jay Naidoo told me that people working on inequality are relearning now that 'power is built at the grassroots, and so we're getting back down to the ground, back to organizing, village by village, street by street. The future belongs to the organized.'

This is not just about marches. Marches are just one part of mobilizing and mobilizing is just one part of organizing. Organizing is about the whole process, about what is done in between the most visible moments. It is about people forming groups together so that they can be strong enough to take action and they are harder to ignore, suppress or exploit, because they have collective power. And when people win victories in the fight against inequality, they still need to stay organized in order to prevent progress being reversed.

Organizing continuously fosters leadership, helping to catalyse the conditions for change. Mexican community organizer Paola Payró, taking me around the alleys of Guadalajara's informal settlements, explained to me how

> when we form a group is when we start to be able to confront inequalities. It is from forming groups that we

build the confidence in our sense that it's not OK to be
left without services, that we don't have to accept as
natural to live in fear of violence. We realize that we are
not crazy, that we have rights, and that we can challenge
those who push us around because we are a group
which have each other's backs. We don't learn this from
courses but from doing it, from being in it. We learn it
when we think with our whole bodies, when we walk
together down the street and when we sit down together
to develop our own agenda.

The form may vary, but the key point is that being
in the group enhances people's collective strength
and capability. As Marshall Ganz explained to me,
community-up organizing is the micro change that
is essential for the macro change. The big societal
challenge of inequality, and the personal story of how
each of us can challenge inequality in our own lives,
are two parts of the same story. Grassroots organizers
I have come to know show this: people organizing in
Central America to prevent violence against women;
campaigners against land grabs in Cambodia; organizers in Zambia pushing multinational corporations
to pay their fair share of tax; Australian Aboriginal
communities demanding justice from companies that
pollute the rivers on which they depend.

In a ragpickers slum in Delhi, I sat with an amazing
group of women and girl leaders who have found that
together they have power. 'We used to be so shy, I would
not go out or speak like this, but then one person, then
another, then another, and then more got involved.
Schools are our right, the right of every person – and
yet our neighbourhood had no school. We campaigned
for a school, then for no fees, then for enough teachers,

then for chairs and desks. We won. We are pushing for a health centre now. We used to fear government officials – now they fear us!'

At the Paris climate talks I caught up with Yeb Sano, the former Philippines diplomat whose very undiplomatic tearful demand for action in the name of the affected at an earlier set of climate talks became a viral video which moved millions of people around the world. Yeb was removed as a diplomat after pressure from the US who saw his speaking out as a threat; but in shifting from the inside to the outside, he'd become a much bigger threat. He'd just walked for sixty days from Rome to Paris as part of a People's Pilgrimage. 'You don't look tired', I remarked. 'Humans were built to walk', he replied joyfully. 'Are you optimistic about the Paris talks?' I asked. 'No.' 'How come you look happier than I've ever seen you?' 'The *movement* is building.' Unprecedented numbers of people had taken peacefully and powerfully to the streets, including in Paris. Faith communities had come together as one to call to confront climate change and inequality. They shared a petition of 1,780,528 people, each name carefully recorded – but most importantly, done together. The people most affected by climate change were organizing, speaking out, and being heard. Having worked on the inside of the formal negotiating process and seen how it works, Yeb understood that the only route to climate justice will be through people power. He was prescient: since then, school strikes and climate marches have engaged a new generation of activists, mobilized millions, and demonstrated people's readiness to organize.

Organizing is difficult, time-consuming and never guaranteed to work. Salvadorian farmer Mario

Ramírez Cañas, describing what it has been like for the community to build their farming cooperative in the face of so much challenge from powerful landlords and officials, used this powerful image: 'we are like salmon – we have had to swim upstream!' One of the best books on organizing is entitled *No Shortcuts*, which is also the best two-word summary of the challenges. A conversation I had with a group of workers in the US Mid-West illustrated this: they shared how they were exhausted from doing multiple jobs, sometimes left as sole worker for 'two-man jobs', and still unable to cover their living costs. On what to do about it, one pointed out how 'bosses don't want unions, but if we all get together we could form one, but we don't get together'. When I asked why they don't get together in a union, however, one said 'but unions wouldn't do nothing for us, they're only in it for themselves' (union organizers call this 'third-partying the union'). Another said 'but unions would not be allowed', even though American workers have had a formal right to unionize for eighty years!

To be a group you need to *feel* like a group and believe in yourselves as a group. As social scientist Alice Evans notes in her brilliant paper 'Politicizing inequality: the power of ideas':

> Self-perceptions may perpetuate inequalities if disadvantaged groups do not identify with one another. Instead of capitalizing on their greatest asset (numerical strength), marginalized groups may rely on vertical ties of elite patronage and guidance. If domestic workers do not interact, they may not develop solidarity. Similarly, in Bolivia, before the 1980s, ethnic groups in the lowland and highland regions did not always identify

as 'indigenous'; they did not perceive themselves as relevantly alike.

But though organizing is hard, it is not impossible. The inequality crisis has precipitated a resurgence of social movements that echo and learn from the past, but also build from it, often led by the young: they are showing what is possible through the claiming of political space by oppressed people to confront unjust power relationships, and what can be done, even in the face of entrenched historical and social inequality, to work towards societies where everyone is important.

We've seen glimpses of what is possible, of what progress in the fight against inequality already looks like: the mobilization of a million farmers in Uganda against taxes on agricultural inputs; the ending of VAT on bread in Zambia; the handing back of land illegally acquired in Cambodia; the expansion of primary education across Africa; the growing challenge to austerity in Europe; the resurgence of racial justice activism in the US led by the Black Lives Matter movement; developing countries insisting that compensation for loss and damage be part of the deal on climate change. In Nigeria, Senegal and South Africa, organizing by trade unions has secured increases in minimum wages. Inspired by the great campaigns of old – anti-slavery, anti-colonialism, votes for women, anti-apartheid, drop the debt – determined people of today are building collective power that can shift power out of the grip of elites.

It is sometimes argued that people can't organize in the informal sector, but in the industrial age the dockers were initially piece workers, and informal sector organizing is building again today, with successes from West

Africa to India, building on trade unionism's history and coupling it with learning from and working side by side with other social movements. It is sometimes argued too that 'technology' renders certain jobs inevitably unorganizable. The successful organizing of strikes by Uber, Lyft and Deliveroo drivers show that to be a fiction – a fiction *created* to weaken workers. Alison Hirsh at the Service Employees International Union (SEIU) shared what they have learnt from their support of cleaners, private security and food delivery workers to organize: 'There is no category of work, there is no app, that means that some jobs can't be unionized. *Any* job can be a good union job, you just need to build the union.'

Though the fight against inequality starts with particular struggles, it can't end there. This is partly about the importance of sheer numbers. As Kingian organizer Charles Alphin likes to say, 'leadership means leaders with *ships*, not with *canoes*!' It is also about the power of what each group brings: the scale of challenge means that no organization, and no sector of organizations, can win this fight on its own. Advancing inclusive societies cannot be done by any one organization alone but requires broad and deeply-rooted coalitions to generate the conditions for transformation. Emad Emam, reflecting on organizing across North Africa, highlights how 'movements that are vibrant but scattered' are not strong enough to challenge the dominance of the economy and society by the elite: 'fragmentation is how we are kept vulnerable'.

The different groups, each with their own struggles, bring a vital rootedness and diversity, but must not be separate streams of activity, but be part of a collective effort to show the powerful that people will not stand for the continued concentration of power and wealth in the hands of the few. As Thea Lee explained to me, 'one of the keys is to build a broad-based coalition, so that we don't get groups that can be played off against each other. If workers, or women, or people of colour, or immigrant rights activists, are all in their separate silos, we're probably not going to win this battle, but if we all come together and we find the common ground across all those organizations, then we have a fighting chance at building the kind of coalition that can build political power, build grassroots power, and really make a difference.' That's why it's so key that unions are strengthening partnerships to help organize unemployed people and informal workers who might not initially see their jobs as unionizable, and to help organize professionals who might not see themselves initially as 'workers'.

An old slogan of mobilizers goes: 'the people united will never be defeated.' In fact, the people united are *often* defeated, but the people divided are *always* defeated. The organizing work to fight inequality is taking on a particularly challenging goal. It's taking on the very substantial power of elites – any organizing approach that *doesn't* link and connect different struggles and *doesn't* connect different types of organizations, *can't* win. As ActionAid's Adriano Campolina recalled, 'every single moment when we defeated power, we did so working together – NGOs, unions, social movements – united'. The Revd William Barber calls these movements 'fusion coalitions' because their power comes from bringing so many different groups together.

105

An effective coalition against inequality needs to be an embracive one. Rakesh Rajani speaks of 'the need both to organize "our own" and also to go beyond that, as only by reaching beyond our core base and speaking for ideals that can resonate with a majority can we develop coalitions that ultimately win'. Economist Andy Sumner points out how transformative change has often connected the middle class and the poor challenging elites together, and highlights the importance of what he calls the 'catalytic class', that has roots in the cities and better access to education, but that still loses out from the concentration of wealth and power in the hands of the one per cent. They belong on our side. Likewise, Nicholas Colloff emphasizes the importance of faith communities to bringing change and the 'disconnect between where the masses of people are – church and mosque – and some of the secular world of social change.'

Developing coalitions of this size requires working in ways that leave egos and logos behind. Building collective power means being willing to swarm. One of the oldest reasons organizations give for not taking up an issue – 'But others are doing it' – becomes instead a reason to join in and help them get further. Dinah Musindarwezo notes how 'we can get focused on our own organizations rather than sharing; you can't build a broad alliance that way as many groups will say "that's not my issue".'

The task is to link issues and movements in a common platform that is intersectional and interconnected. It's a big agenda that connects women's rights, work, public services and tax, land and climate change, and needs a coalition broad enough to include all these and big enough to win on them. The leaders in this context are not 'conductors' – the 'musicians' of change are not waiting for that – but are rather doing something more like jazz, jam, supporting people in coming together.

'When I study history', Poor People's Campaign Co-chair Liz Theoharis shared, 'I see that when there is deep inequality, it is when those that are most impacted by that inequality come forward to lead not just one plan, not just one programme, not just one policy, but a movement, that that is how you get out of inequality. So what is most important is that there is a movement rising up, to get at the root, not just the leaves and branches of inequality.'

Old divides between demarcated groups need to be broken down if a winning coalition is to be formed. The Usawa ('Equality') Festival in Nairobi is deliberate in its process of bringing together rural and urban, young and old, of all communities, in a common celebration and in a common process of planning, because only by breaking down barriers and building community can they build the unity needed for change. So, too, the dividing line between unions and social movements has never been a hard one when they have been at their most effective. The South African movement of communities affected by mining, MACUA, has formed close bonds with mine workers, and been able to move beyond what can be a mutually-weakening community–worker divide to build collective pressure to challenge the mining corporations who for too long have not honoured their responsibilities to either workers or communities. The movement against water privatization in El Salvador has been effective, its leaders shared with me, only because it brought together such a broad range of social movements, organizations, academics, residents groups, and the church – a narrower coalition would not have been strong enough to win.

NGOs can and do get important wins, of course, but when we search through the history of big transformative changes in society – how apartheid was defeated, how LGBT people secured key rights, how billions of debt was cancelled, how women got the vote, how colonies secured independence, how mass legal slavery was ended – we can never point to one NGO and say 'they did it'. All have involved broad movements, the building of power from below and solidarity across. 'Too many formal organizations have lost their connection with society and lost the ability to help people organize – that has meant that they have become victims of popular scepticism of formal institutions', Brazilian activist Pedro Telles shared. As one organizer put it to me, 'we grassroots groups are often assumed by more formalized organizations not to understand how change happens – actually we just don't know how to write it down well in nice English in a document; we understand how change happens very well.' An elite group of advocates or campaigners can't win a fight against inequality.

In my own work in social justice, I saw this early on, then let myself lose sight of it, and then had to relearn it. Having left England to live as the only white resident in a black township in South Africa as a teacher and ANC activist, just after the end of apartheid, I was able to learn from my friends about how, through determined and painful struggle, the most brutal exclusion had been overcome, and also about the ongoing challenges still faced, and how popular movements were the real drivers of change. I saw this again doing grassroots work with communities in India, the Netherlands and the UK. But in my later, more professionalized career, in international NGOs, I picked up those organizations' bad habits as well as their good, and so have had to unlearn the notion that individual NGOs, through their own advocacy or campaigns, can bring transformative change. The arrogance enabled by the power of NGOs compared with social movements, by my privilege, and by the label of professional, blinded me from these truths: the most important change isn't brought by the professionals but by the amateurs; and no one has been saved by others, only saved by themselves, together. As friends from Nairobi's Kibera slum who stopped the demolition of their homes replied when I asked them how they did it, 'we had no other home to go to.' The people who organize are the ones who can bring change: ordinary people doing extraordinary things, the dispossessed, marginalized or ignored, taking on those in power.

To be able to transform society, organizations need to transform themselves so power is shared more democratically, and accountability is stronger. This means giving up some of the power over others that comes with money and bureaucracy. That is the only way to strengthen the most important form of power: the power, with others, to change the world. Those who are not the grassroots but seek to support change – for example, large NGOs or foundations – need to humble themselves if they are to be helpful. In such a position, with access to resources and influence but not rooted in community, they need to support grassroots groups in their leadership, not insist on the direction being their own.

How we'll win the fight against inequality again

No one can 'develop' other people: but we can accompany each other in our respective struggles against inequality. As Aboriginal activist Lilla Watson remarked, 'if you have come here to help me, you are wasting your time, but if you have come because your liberation is bound up with mine, then let us work together.'

There is no one-off easy route to change. 'You can't take the elevator', community organizer Charles Alphin notes, 'you have to take the stairs'. The process of building power together is a process: what can seem as sudden breakthroughs are in fact the result of longer-term build-ups, often of much less high-profile, less dramatic, less romantic work. Moments of opportunity come but can only be seized by the prepared, those who have spent time working seemingly 'without results'. The fight against inequality is non-linear – there will be moments of great progress, but also of drudging delay, defeats, reversals and despair. Martin Luther King noted how the civil rights movement learnt by doing: 'many of the things not cleared up intellectually were solved in the sphere of practical action'.

Kumi Naidoo told me about the friend from youth – a fellow anti-apartheid activist – who was later killed by the security forces and whose courage has continued to be Kumi's inspiration. One day his friend asked him whether he was willing to give the most precious thing he had to the struggle for justice. 'Yes', Kumi said, misunderstanding his friend, 'I am. I am willing to give my life.' 'No', his friend corrected him, 'I'm not asking you to give your life, I am challenging you to something even bigger than giving your life: giving *the rest of* your life.'

Get involved, and stay involved. It is a cycle, not a finite sequence of steps. To fight inequality is to commit for the long term. There is no single policy victory that on its own will ensure that inequality is reduced, and even when inequality is brought down, vigilance will continue to be needed to hold back those who would seek to increase it again. As Audre Lorde noted, 'revolution is not a one-time event.'

Another unlearning I have had to go through is that of unlearning impatience. I am an activist because I want to change the world, but also, I now recognize, because I am hyper-active, celebrating the attitude that 'philosophers have analysed the world, but the point is to change it.' Taking time out to read, reflect and write this book was for me a departure from this kind of 'doing', learning from older activists that change is long-term work and that when our progress hits an obstruction, the answer is not just to go at it faster but is to reflect, learn and adapt.

NGO campaigns often use the language that 'this is a crucial year' or 'this is a key meeting', but justice doesn't come just because there is a meeting, or a moment; it comes when there is momentum from a movement. We need to move beyond the short term, and expand our notions of time. Reducing inequality cannot be done through a quick fix or a short campaign; it is a 'generational' struggle. Part of ensuring that our futures surpass the present is to rediscover lessons of our ancestors. We need to go deeper than tactics and ask how did older generations manage in tough times. Let us re-read about those who fought slavery and colonialism, let us re-read the great stories about hope under Babylonian captivity. Older worldviews have demonstrated a capacity to walk through the valley of death without fear. More recent approaches have implied that with an 'X' at election time and a click for every crisis, things would only get better. This was wrong. There is a need to relearn the capacity for long-haul struggle. Because inequality is structural, this is a long game, a movement beyond moments.

It may well be that a major breakthrough on tackling inequality will come only after a crisis. This does not mean, however, that those seeking action against inequality can 'wait' for such a moment, still less assume that the current Covid-19 crisis, awful as it is, will at least result in greater equality. While crises help facilitate change, they don't determine on their own the nature of that change. What matters is how effectively we organize. The 2008 crash, which 'should' have led to a resurgent progressive movement internationally, was instead more marked by the rise of the far right and the mainstreaming of xenophobic politics. That the world has just been shaken by Covid-19, and that other further shocks will come, does not assure us of overcoming inequality. So we need the patience of being able to keep organizing even if immediate results do not follow, but we also need the sense of urgency that tells us, since we do not know when moments of possibility will arrive, that we have to start now. As economist Richard Murphy put it to me, before the Covid-19 crisis hit:

> Having a plan and having a platform is not enough until you also have the crisis moment – but likewise, the crisis moment won't be enough to shift things your way unless you have a plan and platform. Crucially, these need to be strongly in place before the crisis moment, it

can't be assembled then. The 2008 financial crash was not enough – partly because elite power is so strong and partly because we weren't prepared enough.

Even if we do have a strong plan and strong platform, we might not win, but we might. We know we can increase our chances. So we have a duty to try. Can we find our way from where we are at to where we need to be before there is massive violence, huge economic damage and the undermining of democracy?

It is through being organized that we can ensure that when crises come we can harness them to take on inequality.

We are not at a point of having to 'start' movements against inequality. We are at the point where movements need more of us to ensure that together we win. We have seen for a while how organizations individually raised the issue of inequality, while staying in their silos. Now different issue groups are converging in common cause, as unions and environmentalists, secular and faith groups, grassroots movements and NGOs, South and North link up, all rooted in their specific local context and constituencies, but all connected beyond them. Brilliant, transformative organizing is already building up: strengthened, it can change the world.

Naseegh Jaffer, like his father, is a fisherman, and is the Secretary-General of the World Forum of Fisher Peoples. We sat down together, appropriately, by the waterside. He explained to me how his work fighting inequality started from his recognition of the need to connect his community together, and that this in turn led him to work connecting with other fisher people from across the country and then the world, and then to connecting with other groups facing the same challenge.

How we'll win the fight against inequality again

The first group that anyone can form for collective power, the first 'we', is *necessarily* local – but *from this* it builds out, because people find commonality, and because these networks of networks are necessary if ordinary people are to build the power they need to push for a more equal society. As Jaffer beautifully expressed it to me:

> I'm from Cape Town in South Africa and I come from the small-scale fishing communities there. Our forefathers and mothers lived here [in the places being taken over now by large corporations], so we're banding together so that we can take on this battle. We're not taking the fact that we are losing our livelihood lightly. It is something that we have to struggle against, and push it back as far as we can. We've learnt that what we experience in South Africa is being experienced too in Sri Lanka, in Pakistan, in Mexico, in Benin, all over. So what we've been doing over the last few years is to connect with each other, to build solidarity, and to organize together at a global level.
>
> In the same way as small-scale fishers are losing their right to access the sea, so small-scale farmers are also losing access to their farmland, or to what used to be common land. It's the same thing; it is where the right of access of common spaces is being taken away from people who make a livelihood off it, and we lose access: pastoralists in the same way; people who live off forests, and forest land, they experience exactly the same struggle. It's just in a different area, but the principle and nature are the same, where our spaces that provide our bread and butter and our income, those spaces are being privatized, are being given and sold off for the private benefit of individuals or corporates.

How we'll win the fight against inequality again

We find an incredible amount of movement, of solidarity, of togetherness, of understanding, of working out how we can engage all these global forces as a single movement. And it's a growing movement.

Journal: Challenging the power of the one per cent at the World Social Forum in Tunis

In Tunis, civil society groups gather at the World Social Forum. Their causes are diverse: inequality, climate change, women's rights, the protection of civil society space. African organizations challenging mining corporations to pay their taxes connect with European groups demanding Amazon and Starbucks pay theirs; Latin American indigenous activists discuss the struggle for dignity with Dalit movements from South Asia. The Forum is huge, an estimated 80,000 people; and it is loud, with meetings in university classrooms, tents and on the streets, marches and songs, debates and performances. But though many different causes and contexts have brought them into activism, the groups are all finding progress held back by today's biggest structural obstacle to justice: the huge concentration of wealth power in the hands of a few, the one per cent.

The Tunisian revolution's origins were in the extreme inequality of wealth and power: the economic exclusion of the millions of ordinary Tunisians while the elite amassed wealth and siphoned off billions of dollars overseas. Now

Tunisians have freedom, but 'respectable' overseas banks hold on to stolen Tunisian money, and the cronies of the old regime live in unashamed splendour in Europe and beyond.

Mustapha Tlili, a history professor and member of the Tunisian League for the Defence of Human Rights, tells me 'we Tunisians always knew there was a lot of money stolen but we never knew just how much'. Chernib Mansour, a Tunisian trade unionist, describes the impact of austerity as 'like Ebola. The gaps, the shortages in education, health, access to drinking water, are rooted in austerity, so now we are demanding for those at the top to be made to pay their fair share.'

On a journey to the Forum, the taxi driver, Ali, tells me about the everyday hardships of ordinary Tunisians. I ask him what is needed in Tunisia: 'Jobs for all the young people, education for all the children. It is not too much of a dream, it is not impossible.' As we walk around the forum, NGO worker Rym Khadhraoui, who grew up in France but felt she 'had to return to Tunisia after the revolution', describes the changes that have swept Tunisia as both inspiring and unfinished: 'we still have two Tunisias, we have to build one'.

In the same spirit, international campaigners at the Forum have drawn on a sheet a map of the world, on which activists from across the world are writing about their own national campaigns challenging the powerful: 'Same Planet', reads the map, 'Same Struggle'.

Activists exchange stories of how, across the world, efforts to tackle poverty are being undermined by the power of elites to avoid taxes; efforts to agree international action to stop runaway climate change are being undermined by the power of the fossil fuel corporations to obstruct controls. And when people try to defend their rights, they face an increasingly repressive response: the current imbalance of power means that many governments, who should be overseeing corporations and protecting citizens, are instead protecting corporations and overseeing citizens.

Global NGOs ActionAid, Greenpeace and Oxfam, together with the civil society alliance Civicus and the feminist network The Association for Women's Rights in Development, come together to declare: 'The economic, ecological and human rights crises we face are intertwined and reinforcing. The influence of the one per cent has increased, is increasing, and ought to be diminished.'

Though there is recognition of the scale of the challenge in taking on the one per cent, there is also hope. Luckystar Miyandazi from the East African Tax and Governance Network says 'people are getting concerned, getting organized, and getting campaigning. There is power in people.' Hubert Schillinger of the Friedrich Ebert Foundation declares 'The elite see just how many people are demanding change. That is why they are starting to offer concessions. The one per cent are in

117

trouble, and it's up to us troublemakers to keep it that way.'

Alongside the stories of repression of civil society are the stories of real victories by civil society, and a confidence that has come from the huge popular wave of support to tackle the power of the one per cent: 'We are many, they are few.' At the march at the start of the Forum, the Tunisians sing an old poem that has become the national song: 'If, one day, a people desires to live, then fate will answer their call. And their night will then begin to fade, and their chains break and fall.'

Such is the spirit of civil society today, not only at the Forum but beyond it, too. As the joint statement of the civil society leaders declares: 'A more inclusive society, at the service of human beings, is both essential and achievable. But only if we work together to insist on it.'

Create a new story

Winning the fight against inequality requires that as well as shifting *power*, we shift *norms*. As economist Sakiko Fukuda-Parr has noted, 'social attitudes to inequality are a critical factor in the politics of change. Unless inequality itself is seen as a problem, and equality is held as a social value by the public at large, there will be no agitation or support for corrective measures.' So the third thing we need to do to fight inequality is create a new story. Stories provide a 'why' – and people with meaningful 'why', wrote Nietzsche, can bear any 'how'.

Stories help people make sense of the world of the change that could unfold, help expand people's sense of what is possible and light pathways towards those possible futures.

Such a story isn't something that will be built in policy papers. An intellectual argument is part of creating a story, but it is not the only one. Marshall Ganz talks about the need to speak to head, heart and soul. The everyday phrases and images are more important than the think pieces published. As the great American workers' organizer Joe Hill noted, 'a pamphlet, no matter how good, is never read more than once, but a song is learned by heart and repeated over and over.'

In Zambia, musician and activist Pilato uses his songs to question a society dominated by a rich few and to set out a vision for greater equality: in his words, 'our country is a bigger expression of our house in which everyone deserves to be heard, protected and served; we share this house, and we share responsibility for it'.

At the 'Festival to reclaim equality' I attended in Guadalajara, Mexico, in January 2019, there was no policy leaflet and no long speeches by leaders – instead, we cheered to raps about pride in Aztec roots and about closing the gap between rich and poor, sang along to songs about the rights of women, and gathered round to watch the children smash a 'piñata of inequality'. The success of social movements in the passing of the reform of Mexico's labour law, so that domestic workers are ensured access to social security and right to paid holiday, was facilitated by the popularity of the movie *Roma* which has no explicit policy message but which moved millions to understand with greater empathy the challenges that domestic workers face.

(It is even helping to galvanize momentum for greater protection of domestic workers in the US, too.) I learnt in Ireland this wonderful saying: 'History is written by the rulers, but the sufferers write the songs, and in the end the music wins!'

Professor Pitika Ntuli highlighted when we met the meaning of gathering in a circle in several African cultures:

> When people go to drink on a ritual, they sit in a circle and the calabash is right in the middle, so that everybody is equidistant from it, which is a metaphor for the resources of the country, both material and spiritual, and must be accessed by anybody equally; and then when it is church, our people will dance around the priest and whoever is being prayed for, they are spinning, like a rotation of the earth, while they are revolving, moving from one space into another; and if you are youth at a disco you get in a circle and dance, and if those people overstay their dance then somebody moves in to complicate the dance the other one did and do better. That's again a symbolism of power, that nobody must remain at the centre of power all the time, and that power is exchangeable and it is a natural phenomenon.

A good society is about the values we want to live by and the relationships we want to have. The fight against inequality is ultimately a fight to affirm the equality of preciousness or stature. It is at root a moral question, a struggle for dignity: processes of social and economic exclusion break the lives of the poor, and dehumanize the rich – in fighting for a more equal world, we are working to heal society. ITUC General Secretary Sharan Burrow emphasized to me the importance of reasserting

120

the language of values – the values of work, community, dignity, democracy.

The story cannot be the same everywhere because it needs to resonate in the particular social and cultural context. For example, Zambian youth activist Njavwa Simukoko shared in our discussion about the need to directly address interpretations of religion in challenging inequality: 'The narrative that we are a Christian country is used to maintain inequality on the basis of accepting things as God's will. But we challenge this reading head on. Is it God's will that anyone be left at the roadside, or that the powerful are worshipped? The gospels say no. And likewise people are told just to go and hope and pray; we instead emphasize the lesson that we are called to *act* for the things we hope and pray for, that our faith needs deeds.'

The wonderful 'Patriotic Millionaires' in the US – a group of super-wealthy individuals telling the truth about wealth and supporting calls for greater equality – have set out powerfully that their wealth is not only a product of individual effort but is shaped by unfair regulations designed in their interests, and that their wealth now *perpetuates itself*. They talk of how a more equal society would be a better one:

> It's not because we are nice or good or altruistic; it's because we think it's the only way to create the kind of country we want to live in. We want to live in a country where hard work is rewarded. Where good businesses thrive. Where people feel safe in their neighbourhoods. Where parents can tell their children that they're going to be okay – and really believe it. We want to live in a country that has a basic sense of fairness, and where millionaires don't get special treatment just because they're rich.

121

Journal: Inspiring courage on inequality, the Pope

'I'm off to the most radical country in the Western world', I told my colleagues, 'the Vatican.' There was a time when NGO radicalism would have made our collective attendance at a Vatican meeting appear like a strange moment of conservatism. Now it seems like one of the most radical things that NGOs can do. Among many secular NGOs with proud records of critiquing the Church (and very rightly so), there's been an outbreak of praise for the Pope. But we can't just pat the Vatican on the head for catching up with us on economic inequality and the climate crisis – they've overtaken us, and now it's our turn to catch up. They've progressed, but over the past decades we've slipped.

'Finance, special interests and economic interests are trumping the common good so their own plans will not be affected.' Yes, Naomi Klein is here with us at the Vatican. But that's not a quote from Naomi Klein, that's a quote from the Pope's new encyclical, *Laudato Si'*. He's written the world's most dangerous book, one that most NGO policy people admit they wouldn't have gotten sign-off for.

In a world where corporate power has become unaccountable, will organized civil society find the courage to challenge plutocracy? Will we speak truth to power, and speak truth about power?

Even when we are pressured by governments and corporations, even when we are told to be realistic, even when the powerful few offer some of us privileged access or extra funds if we're well-behaved?

At the Vatican we meet the Prime Minister of Tuvalu. He speaks movingly about the impact of climate change on his country. 'Whole islands are being buried. We need a legal mechanism recognizing loss and damage. We are told it is unrealistic. But if it was your country, wouldn't you?' He tells us of a question a schoolgirl asked him when he visited one of Tuvalu's outer islands: 'Prime Minister, do I have a future?' And then he turns her question on us. A real deal on climate change would mean a yes – but business as usual will mean a deal that drowns the weak. I fear we'll look back and remember his speech like we recall Haile Selassie's plea to the League of Nations in 1936.

In the run-up to the meetings of world leaders on climate change, there's a risk that civil society organizations get stuck in the inside game and get locked into declaring a deal – any deal – as victory. A source close to the talks once told me excitedly 'I think we'll get a deal, we'll actually get a deal.' I asked him: 'Will it be a deal that will prevent massive human suffering in countries like Bangladesh?' 'Ah', he said. 'That, I'm not so sure about that.' The scale of change, the transformation needed to tackle climate and inequality, will not come from gentle whispers inside corridors, but

123

from challenging the people in power with the power of the people.

In *Laudato Si'*, the Pope has set out a vision of community over competition, dignity over materialism. The courage is infectious. I'm hearing colleagues from very mainstream civil society and church groups finally getting ready to speak out boldly on how starting to fix our unequal society and our damaged climate means taking on the power of the plutocracy, and withstanding the pressure they will put back on us. 'We've all been thinking it', one senior NGO leader tells me, 'we've all been wanting to do it, wanting to say it, we just needed someone to say it first. And now that's happened. We never expected it would be the Pope.'

And beyond all the technical discussion and analyses and debates, we feel a more profound call: Be not afraid.

What narrative of a good society could we sketch out in the fight against inequality? We could reassert that everyone is precious, that we are part of a community for which we all share responsibility and in which every voice counts and everyone is a valuable part. We could describe our society and economy as something we build together – where 'I' comes through us, and 'us' is broad. This takes on the false promise of 'individual freedom' and highlights that what we do together is central to the good society, both as an outcome and as a process, and involves the building of shared institutions to connect us all – schools, transport, hospitals – not only for those who 'can't afford private' but for all of us to use and manage together.

We could describe the need for a ceiling as well as a floor. We need to denormalize extreme concentrations of wealth and power, and challenge the idea that they are natural, deserved, or unaddressable, or that enabling the concentration of wealth at the top is what brings jobs and opportunity to the bottom. We need to defeat the neoliberalism of the heart – challenging how even the way we talk about issues has become hyperindividualized. We need to denormalize the assumptions that ordinary people are most productive when they are without support – 'on their toes' – rather than when they are safe, and that those at the top are most productive when allowed to live without limit. This shifts the sense of what people deserve from 'just above a package of goods' to 'equality of relationships' – from merely *surviving*, fed and watered, to *thriving*, with humanness and dignity. The important moral question, as anthropologist Jason Hickel asks, is 'how does today's society compare to what is possible?'

A key part of any successful story for fighting inequality is that it needs to be a story of hope – of hope that we can bring change through our own actions. Kumi Naidoo shared about being harangued for being such a downer even by a group of fellow activists. After setting out the dangerous trajectory the world was on, an audience member replied: 'Martin Luther King had a dream. Listening to you, Kumi, it sounds like all you have is a nightmare.' I could feel his pain straightaway.

No one wants to be told that everything is going wrong. It's so damned depressing. Civil society folks tend to respond to this conundrum in one of two ways. One group's approach is to fib a little, to say that this or that global deal which just passed will transform the lives of billions. 'That's not true', say the second group to the first, 'how can you say it if it's not true?' 'You have to give people hope', say the first group. 'No', say the second group, 'the truth will set the people free, even if at first it pisses them off.' This can feel like a choice between Prozac and depression.

But we can tell the truth and still give hope. We should not shy away from the real challenges we face. The dominance of societies by corporations and the very rich has become so pervasive that it is a struggle even to make it visible. It is only by looking with eyes wide open, and shouting out that our emperors are naked and that we do not want them as our emperors anymore, that we have a chance of putting things right. But there are hopeful truths too – and the hope comes from the fact that people power can win the fight against inequality. We need not only to describe what is wrong with inequality, but also exchange lessons from the past, visions for the future, and stories of people standing up today. One of the biggest obstacles in fighting inequality is a widespread sense that, however unfair inequality is, it can't be beaten, that it just 'is'. That's why it is so crucial to help people reimagine a more equal society and help them see how it can be won.

There is a tendency among some progressives to see themselves as the people of reason over emotion, the people of numbers and facts over myths. This is understandable, but it is not a winning proposition, and is not how to foster social change. Technocracy will not deliver us. If we have on our side all the numbers and facts, all of science and reason, and we cede to those on the other side all the great stories, all the passion, all the moral conversation, then we might feel smarter, but we will lose. We need to get comfortable and able at conversations which not only make people think but which also make people cry and make them laugh, which make people angry, hopeful, excited and determined. We will need not only to be teachers for a smarter world but preachers for a better, kinder, happier one. The fight against inequality is not only rational, it is beautiful.

'At the heart of what we need to do in response to inequality', Liz Theoharis shared with me,

> is to shift the narrative, tell a different story, show that people are coming together across different lines and are building a movement. I travel around communities suffering deep inequality, but what gives me hope is that folks who are impacted by inequality, whose lives are at risk are coming together across geography, across race, across gender, and calling for and building a movement, and not just crying out in the darkness, but bringing people to the light and showing that a powerful, non-violent, direct action movement is growing, and it's when a fusion movement comes together that unites with our moral values, that we are able to have change; and I see that change emerging now.

Conclusion

It's time for one final quiz. Who won the fight against inequality before, and who can win it again?

So, who did you say? And what will you do?

Rising inequality is hurting us all. It is holding back progress on poverty, hurting growth, making societies less healthy and liveable, widening mistrust and instability, exacerbating violent conflict, facilitating xenophobic extremists, and blocking vital action on climate change. It is corrupting politics, weakening the voice of ordinary people, and concentrating ever more power in fewer hands.

Elites, who had refused to acknowledge the grave damage being wrought by inequality, now do so. Governments have pledged to tackle it. These are steps forward, but they are not on their own a breakthrough.

Inequality continues to worsen because winning the debate on inequality is not enough – we have to win the fight.

The challenge of shifting wealth and power from the few to the many can seem so overwhelming that we might sometimes wonder if the fight against inequality can ever be won. But history shows us that it can be, and helps guide us to winning again. The victories against inequality secured in Latin America in the first decade or so of the twenty-first century, and in several regions of the world in the long mid-twentieth century, were won from the ground up. Learning from those, and building on what is emerging today, we too can beat inequality. The moral arc of the universe will not bend towards justice on its own, but we can bend it down, together.

Journal: The three types of campaigns

There are three types of campaigns: the lost causes, the just-a-little-bits, and the transformational.

The lost causes can be great to begin with – the nobility of defeat, the pride in being proved right that things would get worse, the Butch-Cassidy-and-the-Sundance-Kid-final-scene moments. But that can get draining. Which can lead campaigners to the second type.

The just-a-little-bits are calls for changes that don't really challenge the powerful, but do measurably lessen the suffering of the poorest. The just-a-little-bits bring 'quick wins' a-plenty (so are good for people who can't deal with defeat), and bring praise from the establishment (so are good for people who need affirmation). And they do help improve lives. But they don't tackle the causes of poverty and suffering.

The transformational campaigns are those for fundamental shifts which change power relations: the end of slavery; the beginning of democracy; women's rights; anti-colonialism; anti-apartheid; drop the debt. Unlike the lost causes, they are winnable – not quickly, not easily, but winnable. And unlike the just-a-little-bits, when they are won, they really do change the world.

The struggle against inequality is a transformational campaign we can win. Those worried it was too much for the public can see opinion polls by Pew and others that show overwhelming majorities agreeing that the gap between the richest and the rest has become too wide.

Those worried that it would upset the super-rich … well, they were right. Some of them won't get it and never will. It's called Affluenza. It led a rich businessman to threaten to cancel his donations to the church if the Pope didn't pipe down with all the stuff about social justice. But, encouragingly, even some of the richest get it. As the wonderfully named hedge funder Bill Gross ($2.2bn) put it in a letter to his peers:

> Admit that you, and I and others in the magnificent 'one per cent' grew up in a gilded age of credit. Yes, I know many of you money people worked hard as did I. A fair economic system should always allow for an opportunity to succeed. Congratulations. Smoke that cigar, enjoy that Chateau Lafite 1989. But (mostly you guys) acknowledge your good fortune. You did not

create that wave. You rode it. And now it's time to share some of your good fortune by paying higher taxes or reforming them to favor economic growth and labor, as opposed to corporate profits and individual gazillions.

Meanwhile our opponents, the defenders of inequality, are all over the place in their response. Some deny that inequality is getting wider. Some admit that it is widening but deny that's a problem. Some admit it is widening and admit it's a problem but claim that the way to reduce it is to further roll out all the policies that have made things worse. And then when they have nothing left, they call us Communists.

The struggle against inequality is an insistence that every person is precious, that we need each other, and that in a decent society the gap between the richest and the rest is contained. For three decades after the Second World War, that was the global and bipartisan consensus. It can become again.

We've got powerful global champions, and public backing, for the strong clear message that inequality has gotten out of hand. There are, of course, powerful and well-resourced forces determined to further increase inequality. But it is not a thing we need the serenity to accept; it's a thing we need the courage to change.

Conclusion

We need to overcome the deference that leaves us waiting for the powerful to share their power, or waiting for an imagined new leader to arrive. Securing change will involve us defying authority and disrupting tranquillity, and spending periods being perceived as troublemakers. Resistance doesn't *always* work, but acceptance *always* doesn't work.

We need to build power together. We know that each of us will be better able to address inequality in our workplaces if we are part of a union, and that all of us together will be better able to address inequality in our countries and globally if we join together in movements and ensure that those movements ally with each other. Beating inequality cannot be achieved by one great leader, one organization, or even one sector, alone; the future we build needs to be leaderful and collaborative.

We need also to create a new story, not just by bearing witness to the wrongs of our unequal times, but by enabling people to envision a more equal future, showing that is desirable, possible, and being pursued by people standing up together across the world.

These are the lessons of those who have won the fight against inequality before and the lessons being relearnt by inequality fighters today.

The brutal, painful, Covid-19 epidemic has highlighted once again the urgency of a more equal society. The damage it is doing is deepening the challenges we face, and it will not, in any automatic sense, generate the profound economic and social shift needed. But *we* can.

The movement to fight inequality is getting stronger. At a UN meeting, I had to suppress the cynical laughter

I felt inside when officials called for 'evidence-based excitement', but on reflection I think they had a point: it's clear that change on this scale will be difficult, that it will take years, and that it will meet resistance from the powerful, but the struggle to reverse rising inequality is a cause that can be won. Of course, there is no way to guarantee success, but we can do what is needed to enable it. As Arundhati Roy puts it, 'another world is not only possible, she is on her way. On a quiet day, I can hear her breathing.'

Shelley, England's greatest poet, wrote these words to highlight the power we have to make change when people stand together:

Rise like Lions after slumber
In unvanquishable number
(Shake your chains to earth like dew
Which in sleep had fallen on you)
Ye are many
They are few.

If you are already involved in the fight against inequality, I hope that this book has helped you reflect on how to be even more effective, and on how you can involve even more people. If you have not yet gotten involved, I hope that this book has helped you work out how you can. As you conclude this book, let us imagine another book to be written in a generation from now, about how inequality was beaten again. To prepare for that book, the author contacts you, and asks you how you did it. And while you are proud of all you did which led the author to get in touch, you remind the author it wasn't just you; it was all of the fighters against inequality, together.

Conclusion

Take courage as you refuse to be deferential. Make new friends as you build collective power. And inspire yourself and others to create a new story of a community where everyone matters. We are the people we've been waiting for.

Appendix: Who can you link up with to fight inequality

The fight against inequality is a struggle from the ground up, so the ideal people to link up with are those around you. The place for each of us to start is where we are, in the area where we live or work.

At times, people in the UK or US who have asked me how they can get involved in building a more equal world have been surprised (and slightly deflated) when I've encouraged them to act locally. They want to go to where there is 'real inequality' – by which they mean a developing country. But this is not the support that people fighting inequality in developing countries seek, and it is a misdiagnosis both of the collective challenge of inequality and of the most important difference we can each make. Some of the most dehumanizing social inequality I have seen has been in rich countries, and not only in the more famously divided metropolises, but in small, seemingly idyllic, towns.

It is wonderful for people who are active locally to connect with others across the world to learn from, share solidarity with, and support each other. But treating social justice as a problem that affects *only* places other than one's own undermines the struggles both of those places and yours. The bravest reaching out we can each do is not to cross the oceans, but to befriend our neighbours. The challenge of inequality affects everywhere, and the biggest difference people can make is in their own community.

Can you help initiate or strengthen the union in your own place of work, so that together you and your co-workers can win greater job security, better conditions and a stronger voice? Can you help build the residents' association in your own neighbourhood? If you are a student at university or school, can you organize your fellow students? If you are a parent of school kids, can you link up with other parents?

Can you link up with people to prevent the loss of an important community asset like a park, or to secure access to a key public service like a health centre, and through that also build up the confidence and organization of the group to take on the next struggle when you win?

If you attend a place of worship, can you help start a social justice group with other members? Can you support striking fast food workers near you? Can you join in the next local or virtual climate strike or women's march? Do you have any time to volunteer with a neighbourhood group – and to support that group in challenging the causes of the challenges they seek to address? Can you join in one of the mutual aid groups responding to the impact of the Covid-19 epidemic, or link up online with local organizations connecting people to press for better access to services and better support for people at the sharpest end of the crisis?

It almost doesn't matter where you initially join, as long as you link with other people in building collective power to tackle an aspect of inequality, and connect them with other groups in different but connected struggles.

Effective organizing is enmeshed with communities: people connect with a cause that is about their group, working to secure a concrete gain against a clear injustice, and *build from that* to something larger. As movement leaders I met in El Salvador put it, 'build communities, not new bosses; in spite of differences, unite to be strong enough to win.'

You don't have to start something completely new; indeed, it's usually better not to. It's much more useful, and impactful, to join in with a process of organizing that others have already started. There are many exciting and growing social movements active at the grassroots.

To connect with the international Fight Inequality Alliance and some of the more than 300 organizations involved across the world, check out fightinequality.org. To discover what's coming next with the climate strikes, look at globalclimatestrike.net. To link up with the women's marches, check out womensmarchglobal.org. To learn more about the trade union movement, go to ituc-csi.org.

In the UK, both Citizens UK (citizensuk.org) and the Equality Trust (equalitytrust.org.uk) are wonderful networks for organizers, and can link you with local chapters.

In the US, the Poor People's Campaign (poorpeoplescampaign.org) and Fight for 15 (fightfor15.org) – which organizes for a $15 minimum wage and better conditions – are great ways to link up with others in your local area. The online portal inequality.org has information on how a wide range of groups are taking on the struggle against inequality, and provides an excellent weekly update.

You might find it useful to take part in training on organizing, as a way to build up skills, confidence and networks. A number of organizations provide training for those involved, including those mentioned above. There are also excellent dedicated training organizations like Beautiful Rising (beautifulrising.org) and Campaign Bootcamp (campaignbootcamp.org), who also provide great online learning.

The most profound organizing training I have done was the NonViolence365 training at the King Center (thekingcenter.org) in Atlanta, USA, set up by Coretta Scott King to equip organizers with the lessons, methodology and principles that underpinned the work of Dr Martin Luther King, and continued by their inspiring daughter Dr Bernice King. It was so moving to gather at that hallowed ground, to be with Bernice, and to learn from fellow organizers from every generation continuing to live out the values and approach of the King family.

Although training courses for organizers sometimes do cost money, in many cases it is possible to get support for the costs for people who would otherwise not be able to afford the training – don't be shy in asking.

Don't feel that unless you can give every moment that you can't get involved. Fighting inequality is not a profession, nor an elite activity, nor a cult. Some people who want to fight inequality may feel ready at some points in their life to dedicate most of their time to it – but many other people, who care just as passionately and are determined to contribute to making change, are also bound by other responsibilities and want to get involved as part of their wide-ranging, busy, complex life. Not everyone can be a full-time activist, and not everybody needs to be. Change doesn't come from a disconnected specialist full-time small core but from genuine mass movements linking grounded everyday people. That's something to be proud of; it's a strength that will help the fight against inequality win. This is all part of being the change you want to see.

And if you are concerned that in the fight against inequality you are going to make a lot of mistakes, if you often have moments of doubt and questioning, and if you are sure that there are others who can do it better, then you are exactly right for this fight. It won't feel amazing every day – but it didn't feel like that either for all those who went before us and won.

Share with others what you're up to. The steps you take can inspire others to take their own, and they in turn can help inspire you. Tweet me at @benphillips76 with your stories.

The power of the people is stronger than the people in power.

Index

Index

Index

Index

Index